# Witness *and* Wonder

Resourcing the educator

Susan Averna, PhD

Copyright © 2021 Susan Averna

All rights reserved. No part of this book may be reproduced or transmitted in any form or by any means, electronic or mechanical, including photocopying, recording, or by any information storage and retrieval system, without permission in writing from the author or publisher.

To contact the author for media engagements or for signed copies, email to susanaverna@comcast.net

ISBN: 978-1-7377023-0-6

Interior design and cover design:
Deborah Perdue: www.illuminationgraphics.com
Editor: Joni Wilson

# Contents

Introduction .................................................. 1
Opening Story ................................................ 5
Overview
    Guiding Principles ........................................ 7
        Safety .............................................. 8
        Prioritizing Relationships ........................... 8
        Co-Regulation ...................................... 9
        Meeting Basic Needs ............................... 10
        Resourcing the Educator ........................... 10

**Part I – Shifting School Culture**
    The Only Person We Can Control Is Our Self ................ 14
    Positively Influencing Relationships through Modeling ...... 15
    No Time for SEL Curricula? No Problem .................... 16
    Wondering about Needs ................................... 17
    Behavior as Communication ............................... 21
    Reading the Internal State of Another ..................... 22
    The Magic of Wondering .................................. 23
    Being Comfortable with Not Knowing ..................... 24
    When Protocols Are at Odds with Values ................... 28
    Reconsidering the Reward System .......................... 30
    Evaluation Is Inherently Threatening ....................... 31
    Considering Trauma ..................................... 32
    Changing Mindset around Trauma ........................ 38
    Contamination vs. Redemption ............................ 38
    Language ................................................ 40
    When School Culture Is Not Aligned with Development ... 41

**Part II – Resourcing the Educator**
    Witness and Wonder to Restore Regulation ................. 44
    Management of Attention and Energy ..................... 45
    Self-Awareness as an Educator's Greatest Skill .............. 45
    Default Mode of the Brain ................................ 46
    Neuroplasticity and Habit Formation ...................... 47
    Experience Changes the Structure and Function of the Brain ... 48
    Posture Affects Mood .................................... 49
    Mirror Neurons .......................................... 51
    Drop the Story .......................................... 52

Mindset Matters............................................................54
Reframing Stress..........................................................54
Who Are the Co-Regulators?......................................56
Boundaries...................................................................56
Not Taking Behavior Personally ..................................57
Empathy and Compassion Burnout............................59
Belief and Hope ...........................................................61
Self-Compassion..........................................................62
Remembering Our Common Humanity.....................63
Isn't That Interesting?..................................................65
Personalized Self-Care.................................................66
The Rippling Effects of Well-Resourced Educators....67
Fostering Relationships with Families ........................67
Remembering Our Biology..........................................67
Blame Is Pain...............................................................68
Focus on Strengths......................................................69
Appreciating Everyone's Unique Perspective..............70
Being Curious about and Appreciating
    a Family's Educational History................................71
Authenticity and Transparency....................................71
A School Culture of Co-Regulation and Personal Accountability . 72

**Part III Practices to Resource the Educator**
Bottom-Up Practices ..................................................76
    Working with Posture ...........................................77
        Signaling Safety .............................................77
        Safe Boundary...............................................78
        Balancing Openness and Protection ...................79
        Root to Rise .................................................81
        Roll with the Punches ...................................82
        Posture of Compassion ..................................83
        Embodying Courage......................................84
        Heart Opening .............................................85
        Letting Go ..................................................87
        Constructive Rest..........................................89
    Eye Movement.......................................................91
        Widening the Eyes to Wonder .......................92
        Infinity Eye Tracing ......................................92
    Body Scan.............................................................93
    Grounding through the Senses ..............................96

    Conscious Breathing ............................................. 97
        Lengthen the Exhale ................................. 97
        Energetic Breath (Bellows Breath)................... 99
        Coherence Breathing .............................. 100
        Heart-Focused Breathing............................ 101
        Breathing Alters Perception ......................... 103
    Sound/Vibration ............................................. 105
        Bumblebee Breath (Bhramari Pranayama).......... 105
        Sounding ............................................. 107
        Singing ............................................... 107
    Mind/Body Reading............................................ 108
    Sense and Savor .............................................. 110
    Embodied Reward............................................. 112
    Resourcing through Nature.................................... 113
Top-Down Exercises................................................. 114
        Power of Expectations .............................. 115
        Impact of Language ................................. 117
        Setting an Intention .................................118
        Redemption Story ................................... 120
        Observation vs. Evaluation ......................... 122
        Identifying Triggers................................. 124
        The Space Between ................................. 126
        Iceberg of Needs.................................... 128
        Behaviors/Emotions/Needs Chart................... 130
        Drop the Story ...................................... 131
        Make the Implicit Explicit.......................... 132
        Shifting Out of Blame............................... 134
        Default to Wonder................................... 135
    Compassion Practices ........................................ 136
        Compassionate Listening........................... 136
        Just Like Me........................................ 138
        Loving-Kindness Meditation....................... 140
    Self-Compassion Practices ................................... 142
        Sending Loving-Kindness to the Inner Critic ........... 142
        Younger Self Imagery............................... 144
        Ideal Compassionate Other......................... 145
        Self-Compassion for Needs......................... 146
*Endnotes*............................................................ 148
*References* ........................................................151

# Introduction

*It* is no secret that schools and the children and adults who inhabit them are under increased stress. There is a rise in behavior and mental health issues in students of all ages, and educators are finding it harder to meet the needs of students even though services and the focus on students is at an all-time high. Educators are disheartened and burning out, questioning whether education is the right field for them.

As a developmental psychologist, I have been teaching about typical and atypical development, learning, and mental health for twenty-five years. I have taught teachers-in-training, counselors-in-training, and others in the clinical and education worlds. But going back to the source—the classroom—and witnessing the experience of being an educator and student opened my eyes to the current state of education and what is truly needed.

Observing in classrooms and offering professional development workshops and consultation to a wide range of school districts—inner city and rural, big and small, public and private—and listening closely to educators provided an "in the trenches" perspective. And though each school was unique in its composition and needs, there were themes that crossed these distinctions.

Educators reported and I witnessed the following.

- Children with trouble self-regulating and teachers at a loss to help them.

- Students with trauma histories playing out in classrooms.

- Systems becoming more controlling with the hopes of getting hold of these challenges.

- A loss of autonomy in teachers and students.

- Teachers losing the enthusiasm that brought them to teaching in the first place.

- Administrators overwhelmed by the needs of students and teachers, sometimes feeling ill-equipped or without answers.

- Teachers bending under the weight of the many programs, often changing, that the system adopts and tries to implement, contradicting others already in place.

Providing information, alone, on topics of student self-regulation, classroom management, and response to trauma was not enough to shift language, assumptions, and patterns of reactivity. This made sense, as in my relationships as a parent, educator, and athletic coach, I often resorted to my habitual patterns and tendencies, despite being armed with theory, research, and good intentions.

Without a conscious awareness of what's happening in our bodies and minds, we are at the mercy of our habits, reactivity, and external triggers. We cannot be available and responsive to others without first resourcing the self. To break free from habitual patterns takes time, deliberate attention, and practice.

It became apparent that without giving educators the tools to tap into their experiences, reflect on them, and practice new ways of being, there would be no change in educator-student relationships, patterns would remain fixed, and overwhelm and burnout would persist.

To support educators in their personal development, I curated and created mind and body practices and tailored them for educators so that they could practice in or outside the classroom. In small groups where trust and rapport were established, we dove into personal histories and struggles in the school environment and across relationships. We checked assumptions and began to pay closer attention to the wisdom of our bodies.

Over dozens of workshops, I honed these exercises and practices. I listened closely as the themes across individuals emerged and heard the struggle and burnout that teaching was bringing to many. Tears were shed as educators courageously became vulnerable and offered their struggles and triumphs. These workshops were as rewarding for me as for the participants as we shared our relationship struggles and our shared humanity.

What started as a simple goal to inform educators on the developmental needs of children, and provide some strategies to better identify and respond to those needs, has evolved into a model for full system change. While I continue to keep the needs of the student in mind, I shifted my focus to the adults, recognizing that educators needed the support to be introspective, to do the work of self-awareness and self-reflection, cushioned with a healthy dose of self-compassion, to be healthier, present and responsive in their relationships, and, ultimately, more effective teachers.

This work does not lend itself to a six-hour professional development workshop. It is deep work that happens over time. And while I was fortunate to be invited by several districts to meet repeatedly with small groups to support each individual's development, this intensive style does not lend itself well to organizations that are short on time and money.

I wanted to share these experiences with more people, but time and limited resources prevented the deep relational work in many cases. This manual is the natural answer to the need. At their own pace and in their own way, educators can come together to do this deep work, if they so choose. They can take their time, revisit ideas and have some guiding principles, rather than directives, to support their growth. It allows for individual differences, creativity, and flexibility in how and when this work is addressed.

I provide explicit exercises that can be experienced and practiced individually, one-on-one, or in small groups with any good facilitator. This multilevel system perspective is a ground-up approach to system change, affecting all levels of leadership and all roles within the system. Every relationship within a school is important and all relationships are improved when individuals practice self-awareness, self-reflection and self-compassion.

As relationships and educators' "ways of being" in the world begin to shift, so does the school culture. As with individual development, this process is not linear, nor does it happen all at once. There will be pockets of change, which take hold and begin to influence those around them. The modeling of this new perspective begins to influence others, inviting them to look at themselves and their relationships in a new way. This approach provides a means for sustainability when there is turnover in staff and can be utilized in whatever way works best for the people involved. And, as was the original intention, it will profoundly influence the lives and learning of students.

When we resource the educator and make educators' well-being and personal development a priority, we effectively support students. Equally important, we reduce burnout and enhance the well-being of our educators. It is with great appreciation for the educators, with whom I've worked and from whom I've learned, that I offer this guidance. I trust it will be accessed in the right time and place.

# Opening Story

Ms. Jones arrives to school after a lengthy and traffic-filled commute. She's tired but in good spirits, looking forward to seeing her kindergarten students. She greets her students as they file into the room and put their coats and backpacks away. Aware of her students' need for movement, she leads them in some exercise and yoga moves, exhibiting high energy and enthusiasm, which positively influences most of the students. She then transitions the students into various workstations.

One child, Peter, is wandering the classroom, again. As is true for most days, he does not follow directions and seems unhappy. Ms. Jones gently redirects him toward his work. As she assists another child with his work, Peter saunters over, holding his forehead, claiming, "My head hurts." His chest is sunken and there is a heaviness about him. Ms. Jones sits with Peter for a few minutes and asks about his morning.

Giving Peter her full attention, she listens intently and wonders what Peter may be needing to feel better. She offers to get Peter an icepack. She is aware that other students are beginning to go off task. Other students are vying to connect with her, and each has their own needs and cries for help. She feels a great desire to relieve his suffering and helpless at how to help. Reluctantly, she sends Peter back to his desk so she can assist other students.

Leaving her interaction with Peter feeling deflated and knowing that she is now off schedule, her body and tone reflect the anxiety and irritation. Her muscles are tense, and her cheerful smile is gone. Her students begin to mirror the dysregulation, and the class gets more chaotic. She is worn down by the daily bids for connection and how it detracts from her plan for the day. She ends the day feeling exhausted and depleted, knowing that the workday is far from over as she will have emails to answer, meetings to attend, and preparations for tomorrow's lessons.

She goes home and later goes to bed, thinking about Peter and the many students in her classroom who are struggling, academically or emotionally, and feels both the desire to support them, guilt that she does not have the energy, resentment at the magnitude of the challenge, and sadness that there isn't more she can do. She wonders whether she can sustain in the profession as the demands are ever-increasing while the support is dwindling. Feeling at the mercy of her circumstances, she sleeps fitfully and wakes, still tired, and gets ready for another day.

# Overview

We can all use some support to manage our emotions, physiology, and reactivity. Practicing the skills needed to stay regulated in difficult moments and to recognize and break unhelpful patterns of behavior can transform relationships. In education, relationships are at the heart of teaching and learning, and the way we respond to others' behaviors can make or break a learning experience.

## Guiding Principles

This book aims to provide educators with practices that can positively influence all relationships, reach the hard-to-engage students, and reduce the burnout that can come from teaching. The guidance and exercises are based on an integration of several theories of human behavior and well-being. Drawing on multiple perspectives that inform best practice in building relationships, such as attachment theory, the polyvagal theory, and concepts from nonviolent communication, as well as understanding the role physiology plays in learning and connection, we can create optimal conditions for learning and well-being for students and educators. The guiding principles come back to simple tenets—detecting safety, prioritizing relationships, co-regulation, recognizing basic needs, and resourcing the educator.

## Safety

We need to feel safe to learn. When there is not a sense of safety, our resources are directed to responding to threat. Primitive and reactive parts of the brain take over and the higher-level thinking and problem-solving brain is not accessible.[1] Our bodies naturally and consistently assess what happens around and inside us to gage the level of safety or threat. We have evolved to read the verbal and nonverbal cues of others searching for cues of safety or threat.

Most of this happens unconsciously as we size up tone of voice, posture, facial expression, breathing patterns, pupil dilation, and prosody of voice. Dr. Stephen Porges, professor of psychiatry, coined the term "neuroception" to describe this process, as it happens below the level of perception and does not need conscious thought or interpretation.[2] Our bodies react instinctively to this information, bringing us into defense when threat is detected and allowing for social engagement when feeling safe. Thus, detecting cues of safety is a necessary prerequisite for learning.

## Prioritizing Relationships

We learn in the context of nurturing relationships. No matter how great a curriculum, it is the delivery in the context of a safe, nurturing relationship that determines its effectiveness. That is because we seek and meet our need for safety through a nurturing other. When we detect cues of safety, we are free to engage and learn. Alternatively, we may pick up on cues from another that undermine this sense of safety and interfere with the social engagement system, thus impairing the ability to learn, in that moment.

We need cues of safety, and thus, our biological imperative is that we are in relationships where those cues are communicated.[3] Nurturing relationships support independence and autonomy. Autonomy is not a negation of needing others. It is a capacity that arises from that need being met.[4]

## *Co-Regulation*

We provide more cues of safety when we are regulated. Though these cues may, at times, be misread, we can increase the likelihood that our students will benefit from a regulated adult. Over time, co-regulation leads to self-regulation as the flexibility in behavior and nervous system arousal is practiced. This internalized capacity is at the heart of resilience. And, while we can build our capacity for self-regulation, we continue to need co-regulation into adulthood.

A skillful and regulated educator can tolerate the varying and sometimes distressing states students experience without reacting defensively or punitively. The steady ease and nonreactivity support the student's shift from intolerable to tolerable, and there is a concurrent physiological shift from an alarmed nervous system to a calmer state. Flexibility is seen not just in the biological mechanisms, but in the flexibility in attention, cognition, and behavior. We create space for a different response.

Many of the cues we give off to others are involuntary. They are a reflection of our own physiology in the moment and often outside our consciousness. However, we can learn to become more self-aware, to become more attuned to our changing states and physiology and how our state is being communicated through our verbal (tone and inflection of voice) and nonverbal (posture, movements, gestures, muscle contraction or relaxation, facial expression) signals. Many of the exercises herein build the groundwork for paying attention to bodily states and shifting these states, if desired.

We are also influenced by others' states.[5] We pick up on the verbal and nonverbal signals from others, which can greatly influence our own states. Every relationship is a dance, and the more consciousness we bring to it, the more control we have over our physiology, our reactivity, and our behaviors. Perfect attunement and co-regulation are not possible, nor is it the goal. We can be good enough in our relationships without being perfect. The beauty of the breakdowns that naturally occur in relationships is that we have the opportunity to repair, and that repair is growth. It creates flexibility in our minds and our bodies.[6] We can always begin again.

## Meeting Basic Needs

In addition to safety, other universal human needs range from basic survival needs—such as food, water, and sleep—to physical and emotional needs—such as movement, acceptance, creativity, play, and fun.[7] When our needs are not met, we look to others to help us to either meet the need or tolerate the discomfort that comes with an unmet need. That discomfort can take a lot of forms, usually felt as strong negative emotion.

When students are dysregulated, we can drop assumptions about why the student is not compliant or achieving and take a curious and wondering stance about the child's basic needs, stage of development, and competing stressors. Instead of looking to change or fix the child, we bear witness to what is happening and be with them in the struggle. We become detectives as we look for clues in our and others' behaviors. Educators have the same universal needs as students and must practice ways of being to recognize and meet these needs or tolerate their absence to maintain well-being.

## Resourcing the Educator

Being informed about development, needs, and the effects of trauma, and learning strategies to co-regulate are vital but not sufficient. We must resource the adults so that we are able to show up, be present, self-aware, and emotionally resilient. We resource the self by bringing awareness to our natural tendencies and habits. We have patterns of behavior that are resistant to change but that are not predetermined or unchangeable. We stay curious about our reactivity, and we hold off from judgment and become investigators into our own experience. Perhaps we draw connections between early experiences and current behavior.

When we notice a pattern that doesn't serve us, we take deliberate steps to do things differently. It is not just a cognitive decision, as awareness and intention are not always enough. We practice a new response. We give ourselves permission to fail, get it wrong, be curious about what happened and try again. Embracing our shared humanity and modeling this vulnerability is a gift to students. Rather than convey that we have all the answers and that we don't make mistakes in relationships or behavior choices, we model our willingness to grow through awareness, reflection, and compassion.

Practice makes progress. We can only resource the self if we practice. The bulk of the exercises in this book are simple but need consistent practice. Not every exercise will resonate for every person. Some will be more useful than others and some will be more accessible than others, and this will vary person to person. What we need at one time may be different from another. We find the practice that works for us and then commit to it as best we can. Some are formal practices that can be practiced outside the classroom, and many are in-the-moment, informal practices that can be implemented anytime. We can build on our strengths or shore up our weaknesses. In this way, we create personalized self-care.

Part I of this manual considers how the school culture is working with or against our biological imperatives and challenges assumptions about why people behave the way they do. Educators will be successful when the school culture aligns with development and needs. Part II expands on the skills needed to resource the educator and the positive rippling effects of a well-resourced educator. Part III offers practices to build the skills of awareness and compassion, maximize well-being, improve relationships, and be fully resourced.

# PART I
*Shifting School Culture*

## The Only Person We Can Control Is Our Self

When I have asked educators to consider these statements, "We are not responsible for our students' behavior. We are responsible for how we behave around them," the responses are a mix of applause to disbelief, outcry, and relief. This perspective can sometimes fly in the face of the school's expectations of the teacher. Most educators are expected to "manage" their students, so much so that there are courses in teacher education and professional development on classroom management. So, to suggest that this is not our job, nor that it is even possible, and that the attempts at control undermine learning, is an upending of school culture.

Teachers are being evaluated on the behavior and academic performance of their students. If we return to the premise that we can only control ourselves, this is not only unfair, it is detrimental for teachers and students. While many school systems claim to value autonomy in students and teachers, holding one person responsible for another person's behavior or performance creates a culture of control and increases the stress and burden on educators. This pits the teachers against the students and erodes the relationship. The truth is, we cannot control another's behavior. And by trying, we undermine the characteristics of independence, autonomy, and responsibility we claim to value.

Over dozens of conversations with teachers, one theme that emerged was the loss of creativity over the curriculum and the classroom in general. Passionate caring individuals with fresh ideas and a willingness to respond to the needs of their students were being stifled by following protocols of classroom management and curricula. Creativity and autonomy are basic needs.

If we are to maximize human potential and model creativity to our students, we must start by returning autonomy to the teachers. Burnout does not just happen when stress is high, it also happens when there is a loss of motivation and inspiration to do the job as well as a lack of self-efficacy.[1] My hope is that as neuroscientific research informs school systems on the limits and harmful effects of control, the expectation on educators will shift, accordingly.

This is not to say educators do not have influence or should not influence behavior. We strongly influence behavior and regulation in the daily interactions with others. Students learn to understand their emotions, self-regulate, tolerate stress, and develop empathy and kindness, not through lectures, posters, reward-focused bulletin boards, or even role playing.

These characteristics and qualities are learned in the moment-to-moment interactions with well-regulated and responsive adults or more advanced peers. Our regulation and adeptness at managing emotions happens in relationships, not in isolation.[2] The dysregulation and repair to regulation through the relationship is experienced. It is witnessed, and it is felt. Our nervous system moves out of and back into equilibrium and that flexibility sets the stage for continued flexibility in the future.

## Positively Influencing Relationships through Modeling

An effective approach to foster desired behavior, which is lasting, is to model the desired behavior and to interact in ways, moment to moment and day to day, which support these behaviors. We shape students' behaviors and nervous systems by providing new and positive experiences for meeting the stressors and challenges development brings. We work first and foremost to stay regulated, as best we can, and to do the personal work it takes to build the skills in ourselves. This does not need to be done "out of sight" to give the impression that adults always have it together.

When we model positive ways of shifting from dysregulation to regulation, we demonstrate the skill itself, and we normalize that human beings become upset and recover. It is helpful for students to see our humanity and know that we have bad moments and days, and that we too can become dysregulated. It is what we do next that matters most—engage in strategies to self-regulate, thereby modeling recovery, and repairing any breakdown in relationships that may have occurred. For some students, this is a much-needed example and experience.

When we drop judgment about ourselves and our students, give up control, and instead focus on our regulation and reactivity, we return autonomy to ourselves and our students. Students are responsible for their behaviors but not as a means to a reward or to avoid punishment. In a safe and trusting relationship, students can seek the co-regulation they need, and they are being guided to be curious about their challenges. They can take some agency over problem-solving and communicating their needs. They don't see themselves as bad, defective, or that "there's something wrong with me." As defensiveness falls away, their natural inclination toward social engagement reemerges.[3] The basic need for autonomy, creativity, and connection are met, making learning more enjoyable for all.

## No Time for SEL Curricula? No Problem

There is an increased recognition and appreciation for the importance of social and emotional development and the role schools play in fostering these aspects of development in children. Schools typically adopt a social-emotional learning (SEL) curriculum (or two or three) to meet this need. These programs generally involve additional curricula that is worked into the school day. They are often didactic, meaning that the teacher is instructing students on learning about emotions, self-soothing strategies, conflict resolution, problem-solving, or communication. At best there may be some role playing or experiential components. While the end goal is important, the means to the end is not efficient or effective.

Consider how we learn to more subtly recognize the granularity of our emotional state and move from a general sense of feeling good or bad to being able to recognize subtle differences between emotions. We do not learn to interpret emotion by accessing a picture chart of cartoon facial expressions or in a lecture or discussion format.

We take in the real facial expression (as well as body language) from others and mirror it in our bodies. We see our own emotional states reflected in the face and bodies of others. We may take on a similar pattern of tension or posture and send similar neurochemical signals to the brain though this intersubjectivity.[4] We then note those sensations within the body and make meaning out of it by experiencing the emotion (anger, fear) or attributing that emotion to the other person.

Part of what informs our interpretation is context, experience, and implicit and explicit memory of past experience. We make meaning out of our emotional experiences in the context of relationships that are meaningful. Nurturing parents or teachers label these emotional states, initially, helping put language to the internal experience. Understanding of our emotional experience as well as that of others is learned in the context of a relationship, in the moment-to-moment exchanges between individuals, through the breakdowns and repairs, modeling, and co-regulation. It is experienced and practiced in everyday exchanges.[5]

Educators are a wonderful resource for guiding students toward better social and emotional health, but teachers need not feel burdened by additional curricula. They may offer a healthy relationship to offset the negative experiences some students may have had, thereby giving them a new way of understanding relationships and their inner experience. Positive co-regulation experiences create a more flexible nervous system that can respond well to stress and free up resources to problem-solve.

As a student who is dysregulated is met with a nurturing teacher who stays open and curious to the student's inner world, the student begins to draw connections between needs, emotions, and behaviors.

Small frustrations are managed because the relationship is safe. Demonstrating to another that we understand his or her emotions, intentions, and motivations helps them to tolerate difficult states (frustration, anger, sadness) and make connections between feelings and actions. They learn they can have difficult feelings but do not have to act on them. When there is a rupture in the relationship, the educator models the repair, providing insight into what is happening in their inner world.

Over time the student gains more ability to tolerate strong emotion and to recognize these states and either self-soothe or reach out for co-regulation. They begin to trust that they can get their needs met in appropriate ways, or tolerate the discomfort, when that is not possible. Co-regulating one student models co-regulation for the other children and enhances the felt safety in the classroom. Our way of being with one another overrides any curriculum.

That is not to say that teachers do not need guidance on how to maximize social and emotional development in their students. But, it is not prescriptive or a curriculum. Instead, it is a way of being as educators are supported in their own personal development. By supporting these skills in educators, we are building educator resilience and supporting all the relationships in our lives, not just with students. This effectively becomes a schoolwide approach as every individual and every relationship participates in personal growth and development. This way of being becomes part of the culture. Our greatest lessons are acquired and assimilated (often unbeknownst to us) when we participate in a culture where the lessons are embedded.

## Wondering about Needs

When basic needs such as safety, food, rest, and movement are met, the body is in equilibrium. It is useful to examine how the expectations and structure of the school and classroom align with typical developmental needs. Sometimes, there is a mismatch between expectations and development. Children are being expected to read, write, and sit for long periods of time, sometimes long before they are ready or before it is developmentally appropriate. This is not a sign of a problem with the child's development, but rather a mismatch between the normal developmental range and the expectations for learning.

For some students, this results in a loss of interest in the work, frustration, or a poor self-concept for not being able to do what is asked of them. The frustration can lead to dysregulation displaying as aggression, shutting down, or overwhelm. Some children will hold it together through the school day and fall apart when they get home, where it is safe to do so. Others will express their needs through unwanted behavior that gets them the wrong kind of attention.

We are quick to assume there is something wrong with the child who cannot sit still or who fidgets in the classroom, rather than asking why they may be having difficulty with this expectation. Perhaps, the learning environment is not conducive to learning. Perhaps, there are underlying sensations or physiological needs competing for their attention or energy. For many children, who have a high but normal need for movement, the typical classroom would put a strain on their resources.

Designing the school and classroom to work with rather than against basic developmental needs for movement would go a long way toward reducing frustration on the part of the student and the educator. Sadly, the trend has been to reduce recess and unstructured time and increase instructional time, despite research indicating the opposite. Some resourceful teachers manage to set up the classroom in a way that allows children to move their bodies as needed. Brain breaks and periodic movement in the classroom are better than nothing, but really just scratches the surface of what we know school-age children need.[6]

Regarding the need for safety, environmental conditions in the classroom are an overlooked source of threat that undermines feelings of safety. For instance, HVAC systems, which heat and cool buildings, emit low frequency sounds that can trigger a threat response in some people on a neurological level. The low monotone frequency is perceived as predatory.[7] The child or adult may not realize that this sound is the source of their distress, but it will nonetheless set the stress response in motion. Likewise, safety drills, such as fire, lockdown, and active shooter, can be anything from dysregulating to traumatic.

It is up to each community to decide whether the drills are effective and necessary toward prevention. When they are used for good reason, we must understand the impact on children and adults. The removal of the threat may not be possible, but when we understand the impact, we can minimize dysregulation. We can be more mindful of the effects of these environmental triggers and buffer the impact on children who are greatly affected by these neurological threats. We cannot always meet needs in these situations, but we can acknowledge them, and often that is enough for co-regulation.

Educators are driven by needs, regardless of age and maturity. Meeting basic needs, such as food, water, rest, and safety are the bare minimum. Teachers tell me about how little time they have in the day to catch their breath and be still. One teacher reported how she loved connecting with her students by having lunch with one or two students each day. However, by doing so, she lost the few quiet moments she might otherwise have. Another reported she was unable to take a restroom break. Respect, appreciation, autonomy, and creativity are equally important. As we shift school culture to meet these universal needs, we reduce the toll of challenging days and relationships and increase the joy and energy that sustains us.

Reactivity and dysregulation are not reserved only for children. Without a well-resourced educator, the expectations and needs of the students will drain the resources of educators. Mutual reactivity increases the stress, threat, and dysregulation in each. Instead of a co-regulation process we see a co-dysregulation. When educators deny their needs or subvert them, there is usually an immediate or long-term negative consequence. To reduce burnout and retain the joy in teaching, we must be aware of and, when possible, recognize and meet our basic needs and be skilled at recognizing needs in our students. Teachers' perceived abilities to respond to students' human needs correlates strongly with perceived effectiveness as instructors.[8]

## Behavior as Communication

Behavior takes front and center in our understanding of and treatment of children. We set expectations for it, and we shape it with rewards and consequences. Educators spend a lot of time and energy trying to get students to express the correct or desired behaviors in and out of the classroom. We try to shape, mold, guide, cajole, and manipulate children into behaving in ways we believe are acceptable or expected for the situation. When we influence others with strong emotion, threat and reward, the result is often short-term gain. And, at worst, it can cause more problems than it solves. Rarely does addressing behavior alone, without understanding the underlying motivation, have any lasting results.

We're all doing the best we can. Children are good at figuring out what adults want from them. They will meet those expectations when they can. They want to succeed and learn and receive positive feedback. Negative emotion, such as anger, frustration, fear, and shame, can overwhelm a person and produces behavior that is not desired or acceptable.

When we only notice and respond to behavior, we often blame the person who is hurting or struggling and leave them even more disconnected and alone. If a student is behaving in an undesirable manner, we must ask ourselves why. Behavior is a clue, not the problem. What competing demands are interfering? What previous experiences have influenced their mindset? What negative beliefs do they have about themselves that keep them from being successful? What unmet needs are driving unwanted behavior?

There can be shame when we engage in behavior that others find inappropriate. When we interpret behavior as deliberate instead of adaptive, or intentional rather than reactive, we are misunderstanding biology and placing blame where blame is unwarranted. By validating the purpose the behavior serves, we remove the shame and allow the student to brainstorm more appropriate ways to get the need met. Normalizing a stress response and what that may feel like in the body—tension, restlessness, racing heart—reduces shame.

When we respond to behavior only, we miss the opportunity to solve or address the underlying need or root cause. We miss important information and often exacerbate the behavior we are trying to address. We risk eroding the relationship because the student feels unseen and misunderstood. Frustration at being misunderstood is often at the root of aggression. In its healthy social manifestation, shame is meant to inhibit asocial behavior and support prosocial behavior.[9] But, without repair, the person can get stuck in shame to where it becomes toxic and produces more unwanted behavior.[10]

Instead, when we wonder what purpose the behavior served, maintain a nonjudgmental but curious stance to what behavior means, we open to the underlying emotions and unmet needs driving the behavior. When we begin to check our assumptions and shift our expectations, we create room to be curious and ask questions. Expressing genuine curiosity opens the possibility of problem-solving together.

## Reading the Internal State of Another

Mentalization or reflective functioning refers to the skill of reading another's mental state, their desires, intentions, motivation, and emotional state.[11] We tune into the verbal and nonverbal clues that reveal another's state. When we convey our understanding to the person, and if we're right, or even close, we will typically see the person relax and begin to regulate. Their sense of being seen and understood is regulating. When we're off base, the person may escalate or remain dysregulated.

The immediate feedback is good information and hones our skills to read that person. It can be a tricky balance to make our best guess while also remaining open to being wrong. So, we pay close attention, witness the clues, and wonder about what's driving the behavior. We can better understand their feeling state by relating to the experience. For instance, we may not appreciate the intensity of disappointment over losing in a kickball game or not getting the desired prize in class, but we can draw on our own intense experiences of disappointment and know what that feels like. We can then appreciate the feeling state. The experience of disappointment is universal.

The people best at reading others are often the ones who developed this skill for survival. They may have grown up in a family system that required an attunement to subtle shifts in mental state. They may be hypervigilant, reading faces and tone to search for danger. They are sensitive and attuned to other's shifting emotional internal landscape. This can be a strength, allowing for greater attunement and empathy.

But, as in the case of trauma, they may misread the cues or have a hostile attribution bias, detecting threat where there is none. We are all susceptible to misreading others. So, while it's a good practice to wonder about another's state, we need not hold tight to our assumptions. We can convey our interpretations in a tentative way, with a willingness to be wrong and corrected.

## The Magic of Wondering

When we shift our thinking into wondering instead of knowing or assuming, our body changes. Our eyes soften and our shoulders relax. It's reflected in the vagal response. This shift is seen and felt by others.[12] Neuroceptively, we send cues of safety, increasing the likelihood that another will mirror the relaxed stance, shifting out of defense and into social engagement. Simple curiosity shifts the posture automatically. Inversely, shifting our bodies to a more relaxed state encourages curiosity over assumptions or judgment.

Becoming aware of our physical state of tension or contraction, and consciously releasing it, allows for better thinking and problem-solving and alternate points of view. Tunnel vision, for instance, both literally and figuratively, is the narrowing of perception and focus. It is a natural stress response in the body aimed to help us focus on the threat. We home in and are not distracted with what is in the periphery. This can be advantageous when we need laser focus. But stress can tunnel our vision when it does not serve us, and we miss the bigger picture and what is happening around us. Relaxing and coming back into regulation opens the periphery and allows us to see the bigger picture.[13]

## Being Comfortable with Not Knowing

Another cultural shift, especially for those in a position of power and influence is to be comfortable with not having the answers or to tolerate the discomfort. Leading a school or classroom is a great responsibility but does not mean that we need to know everything and have a solution for every problem. Being vulnerable and not knowing is difficult. Instead, we stay curious, wonder, resist the rush to judgment, have compassion for suffering, and know that by doing the personal development work that all relationships and those in our charge benefit.

Typically, when I am invited to work with a school, I communicate first with the person in charge of the school or district. We meet to get on the same page and talk about what is in place and how I can be most useful.

In one case, I was hired by the school's principal to work with teachers, school psychologists, and paraprofessionals to support their understanding of and relationships with struggling students. The work was arranged by an administrative assistant, so I did not speak directly with the principal. After reaching out to the principal, she declined my offer to meet ahead of time. I stopped by her office multiple times when I was at the school for consultation and workshops. Each time she was unavailable. Then, during a workshop, she came into the room and sat in the back to watch and listen.

Normally, this would be no big deal as I expect an interest from the administration. However, what had been a lively conversation and engagement from the group, came to a screeching halt. No one spoke. The energy in the room shifted. After a half hour or so, the principal left, and we resumed our discussion. It was then the participants divulged their impressions of their leader. She was unavailable to them and intimidating. They did not feel they could go to her for support or with problems.

I suspected that she really did want to connect with her educators but felt vulnerable and defensive about not having the answers to some difficult circumstances within the school. She clearly cared about her staff and the students as she made the effort to bring in support. While she didn't have answers to some challenging situations and struggling students, her willingness to listen and be with her staff in the struggle would have made a huge difference. I wanted to be that support for her—to listen and reassure her that she did have the tools for the work and that she didn't have to have the answers. Unfortunately, I never got the opportunity.

Teachers, counselors, and administrators do not need to have all the answers. Most of the challenges in schools do not have simple or easy answers. But we stay curious and open, knowing that the power of communication, seeing and understanding one another, and being willing to be wrong, is necessary for working through the difficult moments. When we feel the need to have all the answers, we lose our vulnerability and authenticity.

Being ok with not knowing is a vulnerable but strong place to be. Just as in learning itself, we need to not know, before we know. Go back to the raw data, drop assumptions, expectations, and limiting beliefs about a child or ourselves. We don't have to have the answers, but we have the tools to listen, to inquire, to wonder, and to show up with vulnerability. This humanity is a gift, not a liability.

As humans, we don't like ambiguity or unpredictability. We feel better when we have order and know what to expect. Our discomfort with ambiguity and not knowing can negatively influence how we make decisions about others. The urge to categorize and label behaviors and the people who display them is a reflection of our brains' need for organization. We have "diagnostic" systems, such as the *Diagnostic and Statistical Manual of Mental Disorders, Fifth Edition* (*DSM-5*), which do no more than describe a set of behaviors and give a label to it. It offers no explanations, or solutions, yet we feel better when we are able to give a diagnosis to difficult behaviors as if that somehow explains them.

This false sense of knowing can feel reassuring. And while useful in some cases, we miss a lot of information once that categorization is made. It shapes our expectations, and we begin to look at behavior through that lens. Many times, parents and educators want a diagnosis or label for a child because it gives them a sense that we have an answer. Don't be fooled that a diagnosis is somehow a solution. At best, it can guide next steps; at worst, it can filter out important information.

During workshops, teachers often present me with questions about their most challenging students. It can become a sort of on-the-spot consultation. And while there is not enough time or information to make any definitive recommendations, we think together using these guiding principles.

One teacher described a boy who was extremely disruptive to her class and her teaching. Her anger was palpable while she described the boy and his behaviors. He would hide under or climb on desks when the class was gathering as a group on the floor. He was verbally abusive toward her. He destroyed property. The principal spoke up and asked, "Do you think this is conduct disorder?" She said it with a lilt of hopefulness in her voice as if having a diagnosis would solve the problem.

Though the boy did meet some criteria for the diagnosis of conduct disorder, I explained that the diagnosis itself was not an explanation. Behavioral diagnoses such as this are purely descriptive. They do not explain why the child is behaving in this way, only that he is. The accuracy of a diagnosis could not be determined in that setting, and it is debatable whether formally evaluating and diagnosing the child would be helpful. More important, the diagnosis wouldn't give a better picture of what to do. Giving him that label may stigmatize the boy and set expectations for failure.

A better approach is to ask WHY the child feels the need to hide, disrupt, destroy, and talk disrespectfully. The answer is not "because he has this disorder." Remember, behavior is communication. Behavior is a symptom of what lies beneath. The child is most certainly dysregulated. He is suffering, and there are basic needs not being met. His emotional state is intolerable at the moments when he is acting out. We may not have the exact intervention right away, but shifting our view to wonder about what lies beneath can open the door for compassion and lessen reactivity.

Equally important, this teacher felt under attack. She was on the receiving end of some really challenging behavior that would overwhelm most of us. She needed a way to stay steady, not take his behavior personally, and not let his behavior escalate her behavior, which is detrimental for her well-being and for the relationship.

This child needed support not only from his teacher but from others. However, a shift in the teacher-student relationship may open the door and give him an experience he has not had. It may offer a different view of himself. The question is how can we resource the educator? The personal practices that shore up steadiness in the face of extreme stressors would serve her well, along with practices on good boundaries and not taking other's behavior personally.

## When Protocols Are at Odds with Values

No intervention, no matter how well intended, can be successful if it takes the control away from the individual.[14] Many schools have adopted protocols for handling conflict or difficult situations and classroom management. Rigid protocols take the autonomy away from everyone, educators and students. When a school outwardly claims to value and support self-control, but then gives students or teachers little choice, the value system is at odds with the culture.

Protocols, when rigid, lack the flexibility of responsiveness needed to be effective. They provide a false sense of control and can escalate and amplify existing problems. Protocols with room for discernment can be a guide in responsiveness. The lure of rigid protocols is that they relieve difficult decision-making or responsibility, potential liability, and provide a sense of control in an uncontrollable world. Rigid protocols reflect the discomfort or fear of not knowing. Protocols that include restraint, seclusion, and escalating response to escalating children, do not work.

There has been an exponential rise in restraint and seclusion, despite measures being taken to reduce these practices. School personnel report no other options than the protocols put in place and more and more children are acting in unsafe ways that call for extreme measures to be taken against them. And, while many schools have de-escalation protocols in place, a closer look at the practice reveals why more students escalate under their steps and conditions.

People and relationships are complex and constantly evolving. We don't need to have a formula or protocol that handles every person or situation. We practice being responsive to our changing states in mind and body and stay curious about the internal state of others. Developing strict protocols or prescribing action often leads to more problems than it solves. We cannot be attuned to the needs of individuals if we have a protocol in place that aims to suit everyone. It may feel safer to the people in charge to have a clear path outlined, but this is an illusion.

While well-intended, inflexible protocols designed to de-escalate a child can add to the threat or lack of safety, thereby exacerbating the situation. As steps are taken to control the child, the child escalates in his or her protective mechanisms, which may look like property destruction, aggression, or fleeing, and thus harsher steps in the protocol are taken.

The situation can quickly escalate, and the blame is placed on the child. The child is not choosing the behavior; the child is reacting to threat. We are not teaching the child better strategies for self-control; we are reinforcing the body's natural response to threat and encouraging the child to practice an unwanted behavior. We then justify reactions, such as restraint and seclusion, as the only options to prevent the child from hurting themselves or others, not seeing how the protocol created or added to the problem.

For example, a principal, responding to a call for help from a teacher for a dysregulated child, got down to eye level with the child and told the child to show him a safe body. The intent was to soothe the child with a soft voice and direct eye contact. Instead, the child escalated further. This is not surprising given that direct eye contact when under threat escalates the threat. When seeing the child escalate, instead of changing course, he repeated the protocol step by reiterating his need to see a safe body. As the child spun more and more out of control, the protocol steps got harsher to where there was restraint.

What might the principal have done differently? Validating the feelings and internal state of the child and recognizing and conveying his understanding for the child's distress may have de-escalated the child. Maybe not. However, continuing to do more of what is dysregulating in the name of the protocol is never the answer. No matter how much a policy "should" help or sounds good, if it's not having the desired effect, change course. We need to be able to read the situation and the individual and have flexibility in our response.

## Reconsidering the Reward System

Many schools have adopted a reward system for managing behavior. The Positive Behavioral Interventions and Supports (PBIS) program widely used across the US is based on the premise that rewards increase wanted behavior.[15] Though there is no punishment aspect, in practice, the absence of a reward is punishment. There are times when behavioral models such as this can and do work but never when a person is detecting threat. Students can motivate in the short term with rewards.

But the system falls apart when we have children who cannot meet the expectations, even with the possibility of a reward because of underlying competing needs. When we base praise and positive feedback on behavior, it undermines connection and autonomy. First, the worth of the individual becomes externalized, and the positive regard between teacher and student is based on the student's achievement and good behavior. This is stressful for any child but especially for children who have trouble regulating.

Second, the dysregulated child receives more and more negative feedback or lack of positive reinforcement, such that a downward spiral of negative expectation and failure occurs. Third, the connection between student and teacher is threatened, because it is no longer based on a mutual respect and understanding, but rather on output.

And fourth, both the student and the teacher lose autonomy, as they are not operating based on meeting their own needs but rather by manipulating the behavior of the other. Behaviorist approaches to shaping behavior discourage autonomy in the child, a seemingly desirable character trait. We want our children to be responsible individuals who make good choices based on a value system, rather than a reward.

Students with a weak connection to the teacher will be sensitive and vulnerable to the disconnection that can come from typical behavior management strategies. The assumption is that praise, a verbal reward, is motivating. For some children, receiving praise is threatening because it implies the expectation for good behavior or achievement and that acceptance is contingent on it. Failing to answer correctly, or not behaving appropriately (that is, waiting our turn) results in disappointment/disconnection. For kids who have a weak sense of self, the feedback from others is their barometer for when they are "good" or "bad" and not just that their behavior is desirable or undesirable.

Reward practices may undermine learning and cause unnecessary anxiety and perfectionism. When children have a secure base from which to explore, try, and fail, and know that they will be loved and accepted regardless of their behavior or achievement, they take more academic risks.[16] A child who has been excessively praised for accomplishments and has a self-worth contingent on performance does not have the luxury to fail. We teach children that to fail is to learn and that perfection is not expected or possible, yet, our reward practices send a contradictory message.

## Evaluation Is Inherently Threatening

In education, we evaluate student performance, knowledge base, and behavior. Yet, the experience of being evaluated is a threat to belonging, self-worth, and self-confidence.[17] If the feedback is in the student's favor, it may temporarily boost self-esteem. But self-esteem is fragile and contingent on social comparison.[18] It is comparative and externally based.

For some kids and adults who are particularly evaluation sensitive, that is, they are more aware of the evaluation and have stronger reactions (often anxiety) to it, they will be under constant threat in a school situation. The basic need for emotional safety is not met. Again, the solution is not necessarily to drop all forms of assessment or evaluation, but to weigh the costs and benefits and understand the impact on the student, particularly when evaluating behavior.

## Considering Trauma

Children with trauma histories are often in a defensive state.[19] They may not feel safe physically or emotionally. Their nervous system has been calibrated to look for and detect threat, even when there is none.[20] This takes a lot of physical and mental energy and is incongruent with learning. The attempts to self-regulate often fail and traumatized children are typically not good at using adults to co-regulate because they have learned not to trust adults or are misreading cues from adults as threatening when they are not. They can be easily overwhelmed by the strong emotion of fear and anxiety and react with aggression or shutting down.

What follows is taken from a classroom observation of a child with a traumatic history.

Eight-year-old Adam is described as capable but defiant. His teacher states he can be disrespectful, a smart aleck, but also sweet one-on-one. He is charismatic and likable by adults and peers. However, he will state, at times, that "I'm not part of this class" and "Everybody hates me." He is uncomfortable accepting praise. He trusts few individuals in the school. He will often wander around the room and leave the room, wandering the halls. His avoidant behavior escalates when approached but he will also state that "You don't care about me" if given space. His teacher reports that he was thrilled to spend one-on-one time with her outside the classroom.

Upon entering the classroom for the observation, Adam was standing in the front of the classroom, boisterous and attracting the attention of his peers. When the class was asked to settle into their morning work, he initially sat quietly at his desk completing a task. The students gathered on the floor for morning meeting, and Adam stayed in his seat.

After a few minutes, he joined the group. Standing at the back, he ruffled another student's hair. He seemed to have a good rapport with the student. He sat down next to him and offered him his toy. The class discussed who made others smile that day. Adam blurted out, "I made five people smile." His teacher responded, "You have to quiet and be called on." Adam's demeanor immediately changed, and he began to disengage from the group. He wandered back to his desk and colored. A few minutes later, he rejoined the group.

His teacher gave him an opportunity to show the class his toy. He easily engaged, telling a story about it and answering questions. She put a limit on his playing with the toy, and he seemed to understand and accept the limit. He reluctantly put the toy away in the coatroom, taking his time. He vacillated between sitting at his desk and moving around the classroom, engaging others. At times, he sat and completed a task at his desk, though it was unclear whether his task was classwork or some other activity.

Although he seemed disengaged from the group work, he was aware of the classroom activity and answered a question from his desk. At one point, the teacher explained the lesson and mentioned that she saw something wrong on an activity sheet. (Directing this comment to the entire classroom of students and prompting them to find the mistake.)

Adam said, "Why you looking at me?" He got up to sharpen his pencil. To reengage him, she stated, "Adam, this is something you're really good at, so I'd like you to participate." He ignored her request and continued coloring at his desk. After a few minutes, he rejoined the group but instead of sitting on the floor, he sat at a desk next to the group. At no point did he wander outside the classroom. His teacher noted that this was an exceptionally good day for him.

Adam is making it known that he will engage on his own terms. This control is likely to be driven by a need for safety and should not necessarily be interpreted as oppositional. When he is comfortable, he engages easily and is more compliant with the work. He is sensitive to tone and direction. Direct instruction that he perceives as reprimanding triggers him. He handles the overwhelm by disengaging. He seems to have discovered the task of coloring to regulate himself. This makes sense as he can focus his attention in a mindful way while still being aware of his surroundings.

Adam is in a safe living situation and has received therapeutic support outside of school. Yet, because of Adam's experience of violence in the home, it is likely that he is hypersensitive to threat. He is tuned in to tone of voice, choice of words, eye contact, and other facial expressions and will interpret even neutral stimuli as harsh, harmful, or threatening (or what is known as a hostile attribution bias). This activates his defense system, and he shuts down or flees, disengaging and sometimes physically leaving the situation. Reports of his wandering in the halls fits with his response to "fleeing" stressful situations. It also makes sense that he is difficult to interact with at that time as he has shifted to a state where engaging him is perceived as more threat. While in this state, any interaction would be interpreted as confrontational.

However, being left alone is also scary for him as he interprets it as rejection/abandonment, which can keep him in a defensive state of fight or flight. To help to soothe and regulate Adam, we would avoid direct eye contact or even face-to-face contact in the moment he seems particularly dysregulated. Instead, we navigate a physical distance by reading his cues where an adult can be physically and emotionally present as a way to help him deal with the emotional overwhelm, while giving him enough space that he doesn't feel threatened. Walking side by side, if he is willing, may be helpful.

Relational experiences outside of school shape how a student relates to peers and adults. The students who have lacked warm responsive relationships are the least likely to create a warm relationship with other adults because their behavior elicits the opposite. Their behavior may be annoying at a minimum and maddening at worst, eliciting harsh or dismissing responses. Adam has demonstrated an ability to be warm, kind, and connect with the adults he trusts. However, when the connection breaks down, such as with a reprimand or redirection, he may lash out with disrespect.

It is common for children who have been rejected or abandoned emotionally to preemptively cause a break in the relationship, as this keeps him or her in control. Adam shows remorse when he has upset or disrespected a peer or adult. While he may not be able to repair the interaction in the immediate aftermath (as he has shifted into a dysregulated state), he has shown desire to repair the relationship once regulated. This repair will be an important step toward regulating him and in changing his mental model of relationships. He needs to learn that disconnection is normal and can be repaired. The more this happens, the less threatening the subtle disconnections will be.

All adults that engage him need to remember that his behavior is protective and based on previous trauma. Though he needs limits, and appropriate behavior is the goal, any type of punishment for his inappropriate behavior will only fuel his sense of "badness" and disconnection. Until he has a better understanding of his own internal reactions that he does not control, he will not be responsive to discipline. When thinking through options for Adam, the key elements at the forefront should be safety, connection, and repair.

For educators working with students with trauma histories, the biggest challenge is to not take their behavior personally. This can be incredibly difficult, even when we understand that it's not about us. Because we are subject to the same threat responses as the child, disrespect or aggression, especially when directed toward us, can set off the automatic response of moving into a defensive mode.

We can be more intentional with how we engage children who

tend to behave in this way. We become more aware of our bodies as we engage and become more curious about our own physical and emotional reactions. Moreover, we can check in to see how we may be mirroring a student's body, tone, behavior, and even physiology, and how they may be picking up on ours. One exercise that can help to us to stay open and curious about difficult behavior rather than shutting down, fighting back, or becoming defensive is to create "The Space Between" (explained in Part III). We release the effort to change our mind and instead use visualization to keep the connection.

Child psychiatrist Bruce Perry wrote, "Just as a traumatic experience can alter a life in an instant, so too can a therapeutic encounter."[21] The moment-to-moment interactions between a nurturing caring adult and a child with trauma cannot be overstated. Children with a history of mis-attunement and disconnection are left with a nervous system and behavioral repertoire that is limited in its flexibility and function, *unless* they have new experiences that can rewire and reshape their responses. Without an adult's help co-regulating, they are likely to default to what is known and what has worked toward meeting their needs.

I have often heard educators explain behavior as "attention seeking." Interpreting behavior this way leads to a response of ignoring a child to diminish a behavior. Instead, if we understand the child is seeking connection, as a means to co-regulate, as they are overwhelmed by a need that is unmet, this shifts the perspective and response. We would not ignore such a cry for help, we would be curious to what is needed and provide it, when possible. And when it is not possible to meet a need, we can contain the overwhelming feelings with acknowledgment, being emotionally present with the student and modeling regulation such that the child can tolerate the strong emotion and build resilience.[22]

It is important to note that aggressive or shutting-down behavior does not mean there is trauma in a student's history. Any unmet need or intense emotion that is not buffered or co-regulated can lead to dysregulation, resulting in unwanted or undesirable behavior.

## Changing Mindset around Trauma

Research and theory have provided a deep understanding of the impact of trauma on every aspect of human development from the physical, cognitive, social, emotional, and spiritual. Neuroscience, especially, has noted the anatomical and functional changes in the brain due to traumatic experiences. Unfortunately, this research has, at times, been erroneously interpreted to mean that the effects were unchangeable and permanent and strengthened a damage model. We know this not to be true.

The brain adapts to the environment, both positively and negatively, and can rewire and recover with the right intervention.[23] This is brain plasticity. However, when I first began giving workshops on trauma, I noticed an interesting phenomenon. Despite being careful not to use language to indicate that the effects of trauma were irreparable, some drew this conclusion. The interpretation that a trauma survivor is damaged results in lowered expectations for achievement and positive behavior.

Though my intent was to empower teachers by understanding the roots of unwanted behavior and give them strategies for intervention, some educators felt they had little influence because of the child's trauma history. This was more than a misunderstanding of biology. I considered this a defensive and protective response, as the magnitude of dealing with trauma can be draining and overwhelming and leave teachers feeling powerless.

## Contamination vs. Redemption

Fortuitously, shortly after these workshops, I attended a meditation conference led by Dan Brown, where I had an aha moment.[24] He spoke of contamination versus redemption. Redemption is when a narrative shows a clear shift from an undesired or negative beginning to a subsequent positive ending. Contamination is when a narrative shows a clear shift from a pleasant or positive beginning to a subsequent negative ending.[25]

The story we tell ourselves about a person influences how we perceive them, how we relate to them, and what we expect of them. Our stories are influenced by stories others tell about us. We cocreate our narratives. Educators know the power of expectations. How we think about a child's potential and abilities influences our expectations and behavior and is conveyed to the child.[26] By teaching about the impact of trauma, I was inadvertently adding to the contamination story. I realized that if I wanted to empower the teachers on just how much influence their beliefs about their students mattered, I had to become deliberate about shifting the narrative.

We must make a concerted effort to bring forth the resilience aspect of children, and the educator-student relationship can play a significant role in that resilience. We need to empower the adults in the relationships with these children (and the children themselves) by increasing understanding while also focusing on strengths, seeing the potential in the other, and the role educators play in changing the trajectory of a child who may have had a less-than-optimal start.

While no one person is tasked with or responsible for healing the wounds of a life history, we often underestimate the power of relationships to change a child's life trajectory. We can be a key participant in a child's story without having to be a savior, but first, we must check our assumptions and expectations to ensure we have not lowered expectations or bought into a damage model.

One way I do this with teachers is by having them write a redemption story about the child with themselves playing a pivotal role in the transformation. Being careful not to place themselves as the only support for the child, they recognize the power of their day-to-day interactions and how the relationship can have a profound positive effect.

These therapeutic encounters can take place in a moment, in a day, over weeks, or over the course of a year. These exchanges shape how a child sees himself and what he elicits from others, going forward. Small moments over time can change the trajectory of a student's life. This exercise empowers educators and reminds them of the influence they can have on a life without burdening them.

## Language

Our language matters. It matters in how we conceptualize a problem, how we are viewed, and how we view others. It influences our perspectives and our expectations. To that end, we can draw on principles from nonviolent communication and other forms of mindful communication for more effective communication. Many of the exercises herein address the use of language as well and how our shift in language influences mindset and connection.

For instance, when we use static language—such as evaluative terms like right/wrong, normal/abnormal, appropriate /inappropriate—we are implying a fixed mindset and a determined point of view.[27] There is no room for change. When we use deterministic, all-or-nothing thinking—such as "they are stupid, lazy, or don't care,"—we lose a connection to the complexity of emotions and needs driving the behavior, and to the humanity of the individual.

Language choice could also generate unhelpful states of mind.[28] For example, when having a mildly adverse reaction to someone, if we started cursing about that person, we became more intensely negative about them. If we characterize someone as an opponent, we leave little room to find common ground to resolve conflict. If we see a parent as an adversary and use language that amplifies that belief, then the dynamic will amplify.

Shifting to using nonjudgmental "observing" language opens more possibilities. We identify the problem without condemning the person or assuming an inherent and unchangeable cause. This is not politically correct language so much as a reflection of a mindset that is curious, does not purport to know the answers, and is open to understanding. In an age of the ten-second attention-grabbing headline or talking point, we have grown accustomed to hyperbole as a way to overstate our point or feelings. Becoming aware of exaggeration and more accurately describing what we see without attaching judgment is a good first step toward success.

## When School Culture Is Not Aligned with Development

Aligning school culture with development and needs goes a long way toward plugging the energy drain on the educator. In cases where the system is at odds with student needs and development, what can educators do to enhance the well-being and learning of the student and to enhance their own well-being in the process? This is where our practice and personal development comes in.

# PART II

*Resourcing the Educator*

## Witness and Wonder to Restore Regulation

Generally speaking, there are two ways to restore regulation. Cognitively, we challenge and alter thoughts, beliefs, and mindset, which changes perception and interpretation of internal and external experience. This can be highly effective in some situations, some of the time. For instance, by challenging beliefs about perfection, we allow for a less-than-perfect outcome and avoid the stress and dysregulation that would otherwise come from making a mistake. However, thoughts and beliefs may be resistant to change.

Alternatively, we can bring awareness to the bodily sensations and direct experiences and work to change our physiology through changing the body. Doing so bypasses the interpretations made by the mind. A body-based or bottom-up approach is direct and efficient and provides regulation when the higher thinking mind has gone offline as it does in cases of trauma, toxic stress, or overwhelming emotion. Altering physiology through body practices makes cognitive or top-down approaches more accessible. Both types of skills are important and necessary for well-being.

The practices in Part III are divided into two types: bottom-up (body-based) and top-down (cognitive-based). Many of us are stronger in top-down skills, mainly because our culture values them and we've had lots of practice. Historically, in education, cognition and intellectual achievement has been valued above all else. However, a shift is occurring where the body's intelligence is being recognized and valued.

Social and emotional learning (SEL) programs are moving from cognitive and didactive approaches to more body-based approaches, such as mindfulness and other somatic approaches for regulation. In my own work and practice, I have found that starting with the body, and working with body-based awareness, builds a foundation on which higher level cognitive skills work more effectively. When cognitive skills are not accessible, such as in an overwhelming stressful encounter, working with the body can free up higher-level thinking and problem-solving.[1]

## Management of Attention and Energy

Our attention and energy are our most precious resources. When we are heavily influenced by what's happening in and around us, we are at the mercy of the whims of others, and the changing state of our internal and external environment. Cultivating practices that give us more control over the direction and placement of our attention means we can remain steady and have freedom to choose how we respond to what comes our way. Harnessing our attention makes the brain work for us, as a tool, instead of being at the mercy of the brain. It allows us to navigate the world more skillfully.

## Self-Awareness as an Educator's Greatest Skill

If much of our behavior and patterns are happening out of our awareness, then we are destined to repeat these patterns as we are cued and triggered in our environment. The first step in changing a habit or pattern of reactivity that isn't serving us is to become aware of it. We become aware by noticing—our bodies and our mind—and by staying curious about our physical and emotional reactions. We notice the thoughts that arise and meet the thoughts that are self-evaluative, distressing, or shaming, with curiosity, without allowing them to dominate our behavior or our states of mind. We explore interactions and relationships and inquire with the curiosity of an anthropologist to notice and understand patterns. We can even regard ourselves with gentle amusement for our tendencies and appreciation for all that has shaped us. We don't take ourselves so seriously.

The brain is a remarkable organ. Our brains are designed to identify patterns, jump to conclusions, and create filters so that we can efficiently deal with the bombardment of incoming information. By doing so, we maximize our energy. The cost to that efficiency is that we work on autopilot much of the time. We fall prey to habits of reactivity and unless we bring conscious awareness to those patterns of thought, habits of behavior, and reactivity, we are not choosing our behavior.

We can, however, notice our patterns and be deliberate in our work to wonder about them and choose something different. This requires practice and effort, but the reward is the freedom that comes with it. This enhanced self-awareness allows for more responsiveness to our own needs and changing states, which improves our well-being and our relationships in and out of the classroom.

## Default Mode of the Brain

The default mode of the brain is to wander, and mind wandering is overwhelmingly negative.[2] We are wired to look for and try to solve problems. The brain has evolved to seek out and remember negative and threatening events for survival purposes.[3] We encode the insults, criticism, and negative experiences much more easily and quickly than compliments or positive experiences. Not surprising then, excessive default mode activity has been linked to depressive, anxiety, attention deficit, and posttraumatic stress disorders.[4]

Another aspect of the default mode is that we think about ourselves—our preferences, the past, our identity—and we get caught up in our personal narratives.[5] When we do think of others, we think of them in relation to us. This is the nature of the brain so there is no reason to be harsh on ourselves or self-critical for this egocentrism. The question is, "Are we at the mercy of our biology, or is it possible to make the unconscious conscious?" When we understand our biology, we can work with, rather than against, it. Instead of getting down on ourselves for being negative, or too self-focused, we can understand the tendency and practice something different.

Changing these tendencies takes intention, awareness, and practice. We can take back control of attention and harness it in a way that is useful to us. We can be deliberate about the experiences we want to encode and those we don't. Shifting our attention away from the negative or becoming a detached observer and not amplifying the negative emotion decreases its salience. Similarly, if we stay with a positive emotion or sensation, and amplify it, we more fully encode the memory and can reap the physiological benefits.[6]

The practices of "Sense and Savor" and "Embodied Reward" (explained in Part III) are ways to notice and stay with the good to amplify the experience. We can practice looking for the good and savoring the moments of joy and awe. In this way, we restore balance to the default mode. Setting intentions and deliberately practicing to modify the tendencies and behaviors that are not serving us is a way to counteract the default mode. Practices such as breath-focused meditation, "Body Scan," and "Grounding through the Senses" (explained in Part III) shift our brains from activating the parts of the brain that are self-referential, and often self-critical, to activating parts that are self-aware without judgment of self and others.[7]

## Neuroplasticity and Habit Formation

Our brains are experience dependent. The wiring and patterns of neuronal firing come from repeated experiences over time that become automatic. Neurons that fire together, wire together.[8] We will default to the behavior, emotion, and reaction when triggered as the neuron pairings fire. For many learned associations, this is a good thing. Procedural memory, for example, where we learn to ride a bike or drive a car, allows us to do so automatically and not think much about it. We automate these behaviors such that it frees up our attention for other activities.

Procedural memories keep us efficient, so we do not have to make a conscious decision each time an event or trigger arises. The automated nature of these memories makes it difficult to change patterns of behavior. To change a habit or habitual reaction, when our behavior is unconscious, we first bring awareness to it, and consciously practice something different, essentially rewiring the brain though new experiences. We break the pairing of neurons firing together and create new associations.

This new learned association or automation of the behavior becomes the new desired habit. It is the consistency of practice of a new behavior, response, or way of being that creates new habits. Once the new habit is in place, we devote less energy to it, because the habit that serves us is now automated or procedural. We do need continued practice to maintain the connections, much the way we need continued workouts to maintain muscle mass, but there is less effort involved.

## Experience Changes the Structure and Function of the Brain

Just as a traumatic experience can negatively affect the brain, so can we alter the brain in a positive direction. Researchers at Massachusetts General Hospital in Boston studied the brain magnetic resonance imaging (MRI) of participants before and after they underwent an eight-week Mindfulness Based Stress Reduction (MBSR) program. MBSR programs involve several different types of mindfulness exercises, including mindful eating, mindful breathing, mindful walking, and other interoceptive practices, such as body scan and mindful movement. They also include group discussions and reflection and an expectation of practice between meetings.[9]

The researchers compared the brain activity of participants to a control group who didn't go through mindfulness training. Researchers observed that, after engaging in mindfulness training, their brains indicated visible structural changes when compared to the controls, including increased gray matter density in the hippocampus, a structure associated with storing memories and emotion control and decreased gray matter in the amygdala, a structure associated with stress, fear, and anxiety, including our fight-or-flight response.[10] These structural findings concurred with self-reports such that the less stress the subjects reported, the smaller their amygdala appeared to be.[11] What we practice is who we are. And who we are is not static or predetermined.

## Posture Affects Mood

In the late 1800s, psychologist/philosopher William James theorized that emotion springs from the muscular and visceral reactions in the body.[12] In the 1950s, Nina Bull, who studied body psychotherapy, demonstrated that holding certain physical postures was incompatible with certain mood states.[13] While this is widely accepted among somatic practitioners, cognitive approaches, such as changing beliefs or mindset to shift emotion, predominated in the twentieth century.

The question of whether changes in facial expression and posture could affect physiology and therefore affect mood began gathering traction in the 1990s.[14] For instance, Paul Ekman's research demonstrated that smiling increased heart rate and skin conductance, whereas grimacing decreased both.[15] Similarly, Daniel McIntosh demonstrated facial expression can initiate emotions.[16] Dana Carney and others examined the impact of posture on physiology. Adopting a physical posture of confidence—chest expanded, head raised—or what was called "power posing" increased testosterone and lowered cortisol, a marker for stress.[17] This intuitively makes sense as when we think of someone who is depressed, the posture is often the opposite—collapsed chest, downward gaze.

What was most surprising in this research is that these postures did not just reflect physiology, but they produced it. It wasn't until I started practicing yoga and learning how I can change my shape and patterning that I fully understood the power of posture on mood. When we are stressed, we contract. Repeated contraction over time affects the musculature right down to the fascia. We can get stuck in these patterns. Habitual patterns of posture and movement may influence emotion and behavior response. Because these patterns are ingrained over a lifetime, they are resistant to change unless we are deliberate and intentional about shifting them. We can see and feel immediate changes when we shift our posture or facial expression and see how other people react and mirror us.

In yogic and meditative traditions, posture is an important piece to opening up awareness and focus. Typically, a relaxed but upright position, lengthening along the spine, neutral neck, is suggested for practice.[18] Opening through the chest allows for the lungs to expand more fully, bringing oxygenated blood to the cells. That alone makes for a lift in mood and energy. When considering all the cultural influences that bring us into a collapsed state (desk sitting, computer, phone, or tablet use), it is not surprising to see the loss of energy and vitality and the increase in depression with excessive use.

Adopting an upright seated posture in the face of stress can maintain self-esteem, reduce negative mood, and increase positive mood compared to a slumped posture. Furthermore, sitting upright increases rate of speech and reduces self-focus. Sitting upright may be a simple behavioral strategy to help build resilience to stress. The research is consistent with embodied cognition theories that muscular and autonomic states influence emotional responding.[19]

We can begin to notice our patterning and the postures we move into when stressed. Shifting into a more open posture can more quickly reverse the physiology than talking ourselves out of the reaction. Many of the bottom-up exercises in Part III use posture to alter physiology, which can be used for well-being and for positively influencing those with whom we interact.

One of the benefits of formal interoceptive practices, such as body scans or mindful movement, is that we strengthen the ability to notice shifts in our physical state. Because emotions spring from our physical state, and our physical state can amplify an emotion, we can affect the emotional experience by changing the physical state. Consider anger arising in the body as perceived by tension, raised shoulders, clenched fists, tight jaw, furrowed brow, beating heart, and shallow breath. If we bring attention to the physical attributes associated with anger, we have the power to relax our jaws, drop our shoulders, slow our breathing, and unclench our fists.

This shift in body lessens the experience of anger, opening a wider range of response than was accessible in the dysregulated state. We do not need to "change our minds" or talk our way out of the anger, though shifting our physiology often allows that to happen. We may still feel some anger, and that's not a bad thing, especially as it informs our boundaries, but we can choose the optimal response for ourselves and others. A formal practice of noticing our physical state builds these skills and makes them more accessible in the moment.

## Mirror Neurons

Mirror neurons in the brain facilitate the recognition of another's emotional state. We read these states through body language, pupil dilation, facial expression, rate of breathing, and tone and prosody of voice.[20] We can unconsciously be influenced by another's state of being and shift into that state. To complicate matters, our state may be influenced by the body memories of our own past experiences that get activated in the present moment. Something about another person's tone or expression or a sound or a smell in the environment can trigger an implicit memory of a person or experience from the past.

This is a body-based memory that is not consciously recalled. Because these memories are experienced as body sensations, they are not experienced as memory and feel like a present moment reaction. We may misattribute the feeling state to what is happening in the moment, rather than a memory from the past.[21] Our brains create a narrative to make sense out of the sensations and emotions that arise, giving us a logical explanation, but the narrative may be incorrect.

We influence others when our nonverbal cues are picked up and mirrored in another person. Many of the signals we're expressing are unconscious and unintentional, and we don't always have control of the nonverbal signals we are giving off. However, just as how altering our physiology can alter our thinking, the inverse is also true. Shifting our thinking can alter our physiology, such that subtle nonverbal cues convey something different.

For instance, in his book, *Being at Your Best When Your Kids Are at Their Worst: Practical Compassion in Parenting*, Kim John Payne details how a small shift to compassion influences us on a nonverbal level, which will be picked up by the perceiver.[22] Physiologically, when we experience compassion, it changes the pitch and timbre of our voice, our expression changes and softens, our brain function changes, such that we are better able to read a person with more wisdom and discernment, and it shows in our gestures. It is not something we can fake. The individuals receiving our compassion have their nervous system regulated as they detect cues of safety. We are always influencing one another nonverbally, and our bodies search for cues of safety and cannot be willed into feeling safe.

## Drop the Story

We are reading and responding to one another's signals all the time. Because so much of this happens unconsciously, we are not always aware that our biology is ahead of the meaning-making part of our brains. Neuroception precedes perception. Story follows state.[23] Our masterful brains will try to make sense out of sensation and experience by creating a narrative.

Neuroscientific research has confirmed that the brain will create a story that makes sense, despite the incoming raw data. For instance, split brain studies where an individual's corpus collosum was surgically severed, thereby preventing the right brain hemisphere from communicating with the left, demonstrated that we will take whatever stimuli we perceive and create a narrative that makes sense.[24] Just because a narrative makes sense does not mean it is true or useful.[25] We need not hold tight to the narrative we have created about our lives or that of others.

The first time I heard someone say "drop the story" was in a yoga class. My teacher was encouraging us to pay attention to the sensations in our bodies and to stay curious about the raw data, instead of listening to our internal dialogue or creating a narrative explaining what we were sensing.

Our brains layer on thoughts like "I am not flexible" or "I am not good at this." When we rush to explain a sensation or a reaction—and our brains do this automatically to the point that the story often feels true—we miss an opportunity to see the world and ourselves differently. Many practices that involve noticing the thoughts of the mind or the sensations of the body without judgment or interpretation are the basis for staying open and curious.

In our attempt to understand the inner lives of others, we make assumptions and create narratives to explain others' behaviors, and these processes happen instantly and out of our awareness. Our interpretations are influenced by past experiences, expectations, and our state of mind at the time of the observation, and therefore are open to error. We filter the incoming information and limit our interpretations based on experience and contextual cues.

For instance, we may observe a student who is not completing work, daydreaming, or slumped over the desk with a glazed expression. One possible conclusion is the student is lazy, inferring a trait or quality about the person based on behavior. Wondering about alternate explanations for the behavior leads to other possibilities—fatigue, fear of failure, boredom, anxiety—and therefore other solutions or interventions.

Our brains are quick to label and categorize. Making judgments and interpretations is the human condition. This tendency contributes to our efficiency but comes at a cost. Moreover, when we are interpreting sensation or behavior while under stress, we have even less access to possibilities. Figuratively, we become more narrow-minded, but there is also a literal narrowing of perception as peripheral vision is narrowed when under stress.[26]

It takes practice to drop the story and stay with the raw data. Exercises such as "Drop the Story," "Redemption Story," and "Observation vs. Evaluation" (explained in Part III) offer practice dropping or rewriting a narrative. Both approaches are useful, especially when expectation of ourselves or others is perpetuating an unwanted dynamic.

## Mindset Matters

A cruel irony of becoming self-aware is that we begin to quickly and easily notice our shortcomings and triggers. It can feel like we are regressing when in reality we are simply more aware of the negative habits. This is a necessary first step. We need to adopt a growth mindset for our personal development. Just as with academic and physical skills, these awareness skills are a work in progress and not fixed. We need to be patient with ourselves and remember that these are skills that can be learned and mastered with practice.

Mindset influences expectations. If we buy into labels, diagnoses, and explanations that imply or suggest a person is damaged, stuck, pathological, or broken, we are less likely to feel empowered to have any impact. We know, from research on brain plasticity and epigenetics, that the anatomical and functional aspects of the brain change due to experience, maladaptive or adaptive.[27]

Though emotional trauma has profound effects on the function of the brain, it is not permanent or irreversible. Likewise, behavior patterns can and do change along with the underlying neurocircuitry. Our experiences and our deliberate intention and attention shifts physiology, decouples the neurons that fire and wire together. What is, right now, is not necessarily what will be.

## Reframing Stress

Stress gets a bad rap. That is often because we don't distinguish between eustress (positive stressor necessary for growth) and distress (negative stressor that can overwhelm and harm). In her book, *The Upside of Stress,* Kelly McGonigal, details how stress is useful and necessary.[28] We need stress to grow and change. We stress our muscles to build muscle mass, we bear weight to increase bone density, and we challenge our worldview to expand our perspectives. Our nervous system needs to be stressed (within limits) to increase its flexibility in responding and regaining homeostasis. Mild stressors are a normal and essential part of healthy development, characterized by brief increases in heart rate and mild elevations in hormone levels.[29]

Tolerable stress activates the body's alert systems to a greater degree as a result of more severe, longer-lasting difficulties, such as the loss of a loved one, a natural disaster, or a frightening injury. If the activation is time-limited and buffered by relationships with adults who help the individual adapt, the brain and other organs recover from what might otherwise be damaging effects.

What is harmful is overwhelming stress, or toxic stress, which occurs when a person experiences strong, frequent, and/or prolonged adversity—such as physical or emotional abuse, chronic neglect, caregiver substance abuse, mental illness, exposure to violence, and/or the accumulated burdens of family economic hardship—without adequate support.[30]

Some of what makes stress tolerable or intolerable is how we frame it in our minds. If we interpret the physiological changes from the stress response as advantageous, for instance, and we believe that elevated stress hormones sharpen our focus and give us an edge, we can harness this response for good. If, however, we believe that the stress response is damaging to our health or immune system or that is it weakening us, we are more likely to feel worn out and sick by it.[31]

Similarly, our appraisal of an event affects the magnitude of the stress response. If we believe an event causes distress, we are more likely to have a greater physiological stress response. Our thoughts lead to a cascade of neurotransmitters, hormones, and neuropeptides that plays a powerful role in the stress response system.[32]

## Who Are the Co-Regulators?

Educators need a sense of community. Correlates of burnout include isolation and feeling incapable of eliciting support from others.[33] When school culture values connectedness among its educators, the burden of meeting student needs is lessened as educators are replenished and the shared goal of meeting student needs falls on everyone, not just an individual teacher, counselor.

Though our ability to self-regulate is largely determined by early experiences and the flexibility we have practiced in our behavior and nervous system, we continue to need co-regulation into adulthood. As we cultivate practices that allow us to better self-regulate and be our authentic selves, we cultivate more authentic and meaningful relationships. These relationships with friends, colleagues, and family serve to buffer in times of stress.

Meaningful relationships are the biggest predictor for health and well-being, and what makes for connectedness is a willingness to be vulnerable, seen, and understood. We need the comradery and connectedness that comes with sharing our inner lives. One way to increase the quality of our relationships is to practice being authentic and vulnerable.

It can be difficult and sometimes scary to be fully seen by another person. Expressing our needs, skillfully, increases the likelihood of receiving co-regulation, turning a potentially overwhelming experience into a manageable one. We resource ourselves when we cultivate supportive relationships. Our individual work of vulnerability and authenticity deepens connectedness, and the connectedness supports individual resilience.[34] Both are necessary.

## Boundaries

Though educators can and do change the life trajectory of students, supporting the needs of challenging children can be overwhelming. Sometimes, working to not take behavior personally and to be a steady presence in the face of difficult behavior is enough to give a student a different experience without draining the resources of the teacher. Boundaries and self-care are essential.

Having good boundaries is different from shutting down or disconnecting from another. Good boundaries allow us to remain connected in the face of some challenging behavior or interaction. Without the need for blame or defensiveness, we are able to be with the other while still maintaining our equilibrium and well-being. This takes practice and awareness.

Some indicators of poor boundaries are when we find ourselves reacting harshly, becoming detached, or feeling at the mercy of another's emotional state. But, we do not need to be unduly influenced. The more we practice a nonjudgmental and curious approach to behavior (ours and others), the easier it is to have good boundaries and vice versa. We begin to notice what is our experience and what is another's experience.

Postures and gestures such as "Balancing Openness and Protection," "Posture of Compassion," and "Safe Boundary" (explained in Part III) may all be useful for setting appropriate boundaries and maintaining well-being and connection. Top-down compassion practices also lessen the need for detachment or defensiveness.

## Not Taking Behavior Personally

In the early iterations of workshops, I advised teachers to not take students' behaviors personally. We talked about how others' behaviors are not about them and how children are only trying to get their needs met. In psychologist James Garbarino's book, *Lost Boys: Why Our Sons Turn Violent and How We Can Save Them*, he interviewed boys who were incarcerated for violent crimes. The overwhelming theme across all stories was the rejection and depression these boys had experienced at a young age. Their aggression and violence were the armor they used to protect themselves emotionally from the pain of rejection and abandonment.[35]

Similarly, in an article cowritten by David Crenshaw and James Garbarino, titled "The Hidden Dimensions: Profound Sorrow and Buried Potential in Violent Youth," the authors use the metaphor of fawns in gorilla suits for boys who suffered major and repeated losses, unrecognized or grieved by the children, and not supported by the adults in their lives. The metaphor captures how the violence is the armor used to protect this deep hurt and vulnerability.[36]

When working with adolescent boys, who have the strength to act aggressively or violently, it can be difficult to look beneath those behaviors to the underlying unmet needs of safety, acceptance, and belonging. Their size and stature may activate our threat system. It's one thing to see young children struggling and remember their behavior is about their needs and suffering. It's more challenging when students are older, and we hold assumptions about how they should be able to handle themselves.

It is normal to be reactive when faced with aggression or disrespect, even when we know that the behavior is driven by the other person's suffering. Unfortunately, an intellectual understanding is often not enough to prevent the mirroring and reactivity that happens when the body detects threat. The reactivity wears on us, drains our energy, and often can escalate an interaction. If our bodies read these cues and react instinctively and automatically, how can we interrupt this automatic reaction?

One option is to deliberately work with breath and posture to send cues of safety to ourselves. We can also use visualization to create space for the aggressive behaviors. In a technique I learned from Wendy Palmer, an Aikido teacher and embodiment expert, she describes visualizing the space between two people and creating a receptacle to receive the words, gesture, or other forms of communication that may be so triggering for us.[37]

I've named this practice "The Space Between" (explained in Part III) and like to visualize a receptacle that transforms or transmutes the anger or aggression into what it actually is, which is sadness, overwhelm, and hurt. Then, surround it with love and compassion. This visualization is a protection or boundary against the aggressive behavior but also shifts the mindset toward seeing the need in the other and making it more likely to respond with love, connection, and compassion. When our students are met with this different reaction, over time they break the cycle of escalation, pain, and reprimand that they have grown to expect.

Feelings are contagious, and we are wired to catch other's emotional states through the verbal and nonverbal signals of neuroception and mirroring.[38] If the state we pick up through this emotional contagion is intolerable, it may derail our compassion. We may have an instinct to avoid the suffering (theirs and our own) or to rush fix the problem. This intensity of emotion can lead us away from compassion when we don't know how to hold the intensity.[39]

Compassion training can give us the skills to handle that intensity, to resource ourselves, to garner support from others, to take action, and to receive the benefits of the action that can sustain us. When I hear teachers talk about the difficulties they see in their students, the emotional toll, and the needs for those suffering, they often sound overwhelmed. The field of education draws people who are sensitive and empathic, those who want to make a positive impact on youth.

The flipside of this sensitivity is that the suffering they witness and the experiences they have can take a toll over the years. When teachers feel they are supported with resources and with emotional support, they can act in ways that feed their courage to stand in the face of suffering and take action.[40] If support or resources are lacking, there can be compassion fatigue and burnout.

## Empathy and Compassion Burnout

Whereas empathy is being able to relate to, understand, share, and take the perspective of another's emotional state or state of mind, compassion is recognizing suffering and having an urge to respond.[41] Biologically, we see a difference in brain activation between those experiencing empathy and those experiencing compassion. With compassion, there is a readiness for action and the feeling is pleasant; we see activation of the motor cortex. With empathy, the activation is in the limbic system and is generally reported as feeling unpleasant with a sense of distress, while the stress response system is activated.[42] Not surprisingly, empathic distress can lead to burnout.

Though the instinct to respond to another's suffering is embedded in our biology, we may not always feel the impulse to alleviate another's suffering. Sometimes we move away from the suffering as a protective instinct. Having empathy for another can lead us away from compassion when we don't know how to hold the intensity. In the case of empathic distress, where the pain, anger, or outrage is overwhelming, we may have the instinct to escape or withdraw. It is like we are living the experience and experiencing the suffering firsthand.

Physiologically, when we overidentify with another's pain such that it overwhelms us, our brain is not distinguishing between self and other.[43] Another's suffering may also trigger fear or touch on our own trauma and therefore feel overwhelming. In cases of empathy distress, it would be difficult to be moved to action to alleviate another's suffering and, over time, it would burn us out.

It's easier to feel anger than fear or powerlessness. So, we might find ourselves blaming the victim, shutting down, dissociating, or denying the suffering. These instincts are normal, useful, and functional. We may first need to tend to our own suffering or to give space to that before taking action. The work is in asking ourselves what this is bringing up in us that is intolerable and taking the necessary steps of self-care, first, so that we may be in a position to respond.

It is important to honor the instinct to be self-protective, and it is good to have boundaries that allow us to take care of ourselves. It is useful to find a way to not overidentify with the sufferer so that we can distinguish between our pain and the other's. One way to do this is to take the wide perspective—having emotions about the suffering at a distance, to be in relationship to it but not in it.[44]

This distancing is different from a shutdown or turning our backs on the person suffering. We are with them; we are just not in it with them. Being pulled into the awfulness of the suffering is not necessary or desirable when we desire to help. Having good boundaries can protect the educator from burnout and allow a helpful response.

The natural impulse toward alleviating suffering is thwarted when under threat. In the Good Samaritan study, social psychologists John Darley and Daniel Batson revealed that people who felt they would get in trouble for being late were less likely to stop and help someone in distress.[45] If we have competing expectations, we are less likely to pause and help another. In education, a barrier to compassion can be the competing demand of evaluating teachers based on student behavior and performance.

Returning to the idea that evaluation is threatening, educators may feel the pressure to create a highly performing classroom or cover the prescribed content. This can undermine patience and the impulse of compassion toward struggling students. Additionally, when we are regularly acting from compassion but not being replenished or supported, or worse, blocked or impeded by the system, the result is compassion burnout.

## Belief and Hope

Feeling ineffective feeds hopelessness and helplessness and takes away motivation and energy to respond. Our belief in our ability to respond largely determines our effectiveness. Caring for others triggers the biology of courage and creates hope. Caregiving emboldens us by activating hormones connected to courage and approach motivation.[46] For instance, oxytocin is released, which dampens the fear circuit and activates the reward system. Dopamine also encourages approach and gives us the sense that something good is possible, while empowering the motor system.[47] Vasopressin is associated with a protective and fierce compassion where we may be aggressive in our protection.[48]

In practice, this may look like holding boundaries for ourselves or for others. What ultimately continues to fuel us when we have the instinct for compassion is the warm glow from feeling like we made a difference. We rose to a challenge and effected change. This change may be concrete—solved a problem, met a need—or it may be that we conveyed a sense of hope that things could be better. Imbuing hope is a state that lifts the person feeling compassion and the receiver of the compassion.[49]

## Self-Compassion

If harnessing our attention is our greatest tool, practicing self-compassion is a superpower. Self-compassion is a necessary ingredient for personal growth and resilience. Self-compassion involves treating ourselves with care and concern when considering personal inadequacies, mistakes, failures, and painful life situations.[50] It involves nonjudgment, recognizing suffering, and meeting the suffering with kindness and soothing much as we would a good friend who was suffering.

Self-compassion is not lowering standards or self-indulgent. In a culture where the adage of no pain, no gain is accepted and promoted, we may think that giving ourselves compassion may make us weak, unmotivated, or apathetic. Research shows the opposite. For instance, students practicing self-compassion spend more time studying for a difficult test following initial failure.[51] Students highest in self-compassion are least likely to procrastinate.[52] Self-compassion allows for perseverance in the face of setbacks.[53]

Self-compassion allows us to respond differently to our tendencies, enhances recovery from triggers, and assists us to be better able to respond and repair. Research shows we are more likely to be accountable for our actions when we practice self-compassion.[54] Rather than a cop-out, self-compassion lessens the threat that might otherwise cause defensiveness or shirking of responsibility when we make a mistake. We lessen the need for deflection or defense because we reduce the pain that comes from falling short of our ideals.

If we look at our behaviors, tendencies, and undesirable actions with judgment, we are less likely to change. Guilt, shame, and fear are not effective means of motivation.[55] Being harsh on ourselves is not motivating in the long term. We tend to avoid change when the motivation comes from fear of self-judgment. That is because the judgment is a threat, and threat is inconsistent with problem-solving and change. An internal dialogue that is harsh or condemning—such as "Why do I keep reacting this way? I am always so reactive"—is a barrier to change. Stepping back and remembering our humanity and recognizing our suffering allows us to come back into regulation and be less reactive. Self-compassion cues our nervous system for safety.

The biochemistry of feelings of shame, fear, and anger is different from the biochemistry of compassion. It's easier to be hostile toward our self than to be kind. While we have a natural impulse to be compassionate to others, we find it much easier to be compassionate to others than to ourselves.[56] We have deep conditioning to feel bad about our needs. Having compassion, especially for ourselves, is courageous. Self-compassion is a skill that can be learned and enhanced with practice. Psychologist and professor of psychology Louis Cozolino writes that it is not survival of the fittest but survival of the nurtured.[57] We can learn to nurture ourselves when we have not been nurtured, or when we have turned against ourselves.

## Remembering Our Common Humanity

Deep self-reflection can reveal aspects of ourselves that we do not like or are not desirable. For this reason, it is especially important that we cultivate a sense of self-compassion for personal growth. We hold space for all the thoughts and feelings that arise in us, even, and especially, when they are deemed to be inappropriate or unhelpful. We can stay out of judgment and be curious about our reactions.

These experiences with others that trigger negative emotion or that bring up harsh judgment in another are keys to what may be buried inside. They are clues into the parts of ourselves that we deny or choose not to see or acknowledge. Rather than feeling shame or guilt over these emotions or reactions, we can shine a light into the darkness and look with intrigue and discovery, wondering what is coming up for us and noticing it, nonjudgmentally. Staying curious and beginning to notice patterns in our reactions. We may gain insight to the underlying cause or original wound, or we may not. But noticing the pattern, bringing compassion, and holding the intention to react differently, can shift us.

Bringing the attention to the body experience can be helpful when the thoughts are automatic and seemingly out of conscious control. We place our attention on the subtle changes to the body, noticing tension, a shift in posture, a change in temperature, or a revving up or slowing down of energy. Noticing first without changing it. Staying with it. Allowing it. Witnessing it. Maybe we employ specific movements or breathwork to meet and balance the response. Over time, we slow what seems like an automatic response to its components, creating space for a different response. We are creating behavior change that reflects biological change.

When we practice bringing compassion to ourselves, there may be resistance. Evolutionarily we are designed to feel shame, self-blame, and to be self-critical to keep us connected to the tribe.[58] Belongingness overrides the needs of the self, and we can experience these painful states as a means to keeping us connected. So, as we start to bring self-compassion, we can have a backlash.

When we first dive into a practice of bringing kindness to ourselves, the part of ourselves that is critical, shaming, or blaming can push back hard. Often referred to as the inner critic, this part evolved in a misguided way to protect us. Trying to counteract or rid ourselves of the inner critic can be difficult if we don't take our time. We may feel resistance to giving ourselves warmth as it undermines the misguided, yet protective purpose of the inner critic.[59] It is only after appreciating what the inner critical part of ourselves is attempting to do—protect us—that we can befriend it and give it permission to stand down.

Sometimes, we are too entrenched in the negative belief about ourselves to bring kindness. It can be helpful to step back and get a larger perspective from a wise and witnessing self or to imagine what a loving friend would say. Or, it may be useful to envision the younger more vulnerable version of ourselves, and bring love, understanding, and compassion to that version. All of the exercises that help build the skill of self-compassion have the potential to elicit pushback. Go slowly and see how it feels. Stay curious about our reactions, especially those where the inner critic gets louder.

## Isn't That Interesting?

In the book, *A Fearless Heart: How the Courage to Be Compassionate Can Transform Our Lives,* Tibetan Buddhist scholar and former monk Thupten Jinpa writes about intention and tone when reflecting on our behavior. There's a difference between the accusing and shaming tone of "Why did I do that!?" and the curious but kind "I wonder why I did that."[60]

When we can remember our common humanity and know that we will not always make the best choice or decision, that we will be reactive and do and say things that may harm ourselves or another, and that it is not an indication of our goodness or badness, then we can look more closely at our patterns with curiosity.

In leading workshops and groups on self-compassion, an interesting pattern emerged across groups. As participants practiced paying attention to their states and inner dialogue, and became more mindful, they at first reported a dip in self-compassion. Both qualitative and quantitative measures revealed that participants felt they were getting worse at bringing self-kindness. In reality, they were becoming more aware of the negative self-talk that plays in the background and how harsh their inner critic was.

It took some time to practice the exercises of self-compassion to counteract these tendencies and to be with the inner critic to see the protective value it provides. Getting stuck at this point can be tricky, because if we have harsh feelings toward ourselves for our reactivity then we can get down on ourselves and stop the self-inquiry.

Setting an intention to keep noticing and slowing, shifting, and celebrating the victories, motivates us to keep going. Suddenly, we are not reacting to those same small triggers, or, if we are, we can smile inwardly with a recognition of "Oh, yeah, that's my stuff. There it is again. Thanks for the reminder, I'll keep working with that."

## Personalized Self-Care

There is no one-size-fits-all approach to self-care and personal development. What works for one person may not for another. What is useful one day may be inaccessible on another day. The good news is that there are dozens of approaches and practices, both formal and informal, that can be accessed.

There are skills that can be employed in the moment of a stressful or challenging encounter, and there are skills that we practice consistently outside the stress-filled moments and build the capacity and ability just like we would any other skill. None of these require huge amounts of time out of the day. What is most important is consistency of practice, setting intentions, and following through with the best of our ability, and when we fall short begin again.

## The Rippling Effects of Well-Resourced Educators

As we advance in our personal development and become more skilled at managing our attention, energy, and mindset, all our relationships, personal and professional, benefit. We are able to show up for and maintain well-being with students and their families, colleagues, peers, and loved ones. It is then that we give a gift of a different and positive experience to the students and can authentically connect with families. Our influence extends to all those we encounter.

As we begin to navigate the world more skillfully, we have the means to keep ourselves more regulated and not at the mercy of the behavior of those around us. We don't get drawn into the drama as quickly or easily, we can discern what is me and what is them. And because we can see this as "not me," we can have compassion for the suffering driving the other's behavior.

Paradoxically, it is our shared humanity that allows for compassion when we recognize ourselves in others—the human experience of confusion, anger, threat, or fear—but know that this suffering, in this moment, is theirs. This is as important for working with families as it is working with students.

## Fostering Relationships with Families

Partnering with families is one of the best resources and can also be the one most fraught with difficulty. Remembering that we all default to a defensive state (whether that be with aggression, denial, or shutting down) under overwhelming stress, and not knowing what the other party is thinking or feeling can lead to unnecessary battles. To lessen defensiveness, we start with the basic principle of safety.

## Remembering Our Biology

Safety is in the eye of the beholder. While we may feel safe, we cannot assume this is true for others. It is useful to consider whether we are giving cues of safety to our collaborators. What might be threatening to them? I have sat in on dozens of planning and placement team (PPT) meetings, first as a school counselor and later as a consultant.

It was interesting to witness how the family viewed the team. Some were grateful and trusting that the needs of the child were being addressed. Some were scared or skeptical. Some appeared to feel empowered, while others felt under attack and defensive.

One of my most salient memories is of a parent who, at the beginning of a meeting, slammed an audio recorder down in the middle of the table and looked at the team leader with aggression as if she were challenging her. She clearly lacked trust in the team and was asserting her control. It is useful to ask ourselves whether the family appears to be under threat and whether we are reacting to cues of threat. How can we self-regulate to retain conscious control over our reactions?

## Blame Is Pain

What happens when two parties come together to solve a problem, but each is wary of the other or feeling blamed by the other? Holding an assumption that parents or caregivers are, at least in part, to blame for the child's behavior damages the potential collaboration with families and is often misguided. Whenever we see finger pointing—it's the parents' fault, teacher's fault, child's fault—we can look at our emotional experience underlying the blame. Are we frustrated, angry, scared, defensive?

Under blame is often fear or another intolerable emotion. An uncomfortable feeling is just that, a temporary feeling. It's important information. When we can look at the fear with compassion, and use tools to regain a sense of safety, there is no need for blame. There is nothing wrong with accountability. We need to be held accountable for what is in our control.

Blaming others is a false way to feel in control. The only person we can control is ourselves. We cannot blame others for our reactivity. One of the most loving and compassionate things we can do is manage our own state by recognizing the pain or fear driving the blame and bring compassion to it.

## Focus on Strengths

Part of what brings about defensiveness is the focus on the student's weaknesses or shortcomings. If we are always in a remedial mode, rather than noticing strengths, we do a disservice to the student, and we unnecessarily raise the stress and defensiveness of educators and caregivers. It is useful to build capacity with skills that are lacking, however, focusing on what is missing in the child contributes to a weakened self-concept and a defensive or shamed family. Negative evaluation is a threat that reduces the likelihood of future success.

Many schools have adopted functional behavior assessments that track the unwanted behaviors of a student. Reports detail the progress of a student calculating the number of incidences over a particular time period. Imagine if we had monitored your behavior from the last year, picked the five worst days, detailed the behaviors and choices from that day, and wrote a report describing you only from your worst moments.

Now imagine that report is distributed to your current colleagues and future colleagues who have not yet met you. There's no context, and no mention of all the wonderful attributes, traits, and moments you've had over the past year. Imagine how you might be received when meeting your new colleagues for the first time. It seems unfair and absurd, yet we do this with students.

Focusing on strengths does not mean we deny that a child is struggling. Instead, we see the whole child. We appreciate the strengths, and we wonder about the challenges. We don't simply define, monitor, and report on negative behavior. To counteract this practice, one school psychologist with whom I collaborated offered a "student at a glance" page to new teachers when a student transitioned from one teacher or school to the next. The page summarized the student's talents, likes, and strengths as well as challenges, providing a well-rounded picture of the student.

We know it's important to focus on strengths over challenges. But we are often pulled by what's missing, not up to speed, or in need of remediation, and our attention and energy goes there. When we notice ourselves moving in that direction, stop, and try shifting our attention to what is going well. We can offer this mindset shift to ourselves as well.

Becoming aware of the inner critic and the negative thoughts, we deliberately shift our attention to an aspect of ourselves we appreciate or to what is going well. Giving attention to what's working in ourselves and others is a better use of energy than giving attention to what is not working.

## Appreciating Everyone's Unique Perspectives

As educators, we can get caught up in the expert role and lose sight of the big picture or not know we are missing parts of the bigger picture. We each have our unique perspective based on past experience, implicit bias, and unconscious memory. It is easy to miss information that is relevant because our efficient brains filter incoming information through our expectations and assumptions.

We need to deliberately challenge our assumptions, our ways of knowing, and be open to other points of view. It does not mean we are wrong or that multiple realities cannot be true at once. When we collaborate, we are open to all points of view, we respect all experience, and we aim to connect by finding common ground in our human experience. The practice "Just Like Me" (explained in Part III) is useful for this purpose. Practicing mentalizing exercises, such as "Iceberg of Needs," (explained in Part III) strengthens our ability to understand the parent's point of view, and what fears, desires, or assumptions they may be holding.

## Being Curious about and Appreciating a Family's Educational History

Though not always the case, children who struggle in school may have parents who struggled, for the same or for different reasons. Parents come in with their expectations for how they'll be received and how they need to be to get what they need for their child. Largely influenced by their school experiences, they may be confident and open, defensive or aggressive, or helpless and looking to the educators as the expert.

Staying curious about the needs and emotion underlying parent behavior, and how this may be related to past experiences of their own or their child's educational history, can be useful. We can acknowledge the pain of past or current experience and make room for strong emotion.

As educators, it is also useful to reflect on our educational history. What experiences influenced us the most? What were the quality of those experiences and how have they shaped our view about teaching and learning? What assumptions might we be making about another's experience? Having compassion for self and others lessens defensiveness. We accept our shared humanity and join forces.

## Authenticity and Transparency

It is difficult to convey information that may upset, disappoint, or anger another person. We may avoid these conversations by minimizing a problem, making false promises, or telling parents what they want to hear. Any trust built on this inauthenticity will be short-lived. Likewise, language that doesn't convey any real information is potentially damaging to the relationship.

Organizations and systems often adopt lofty language that is vague or unclear. I call this pseudo speak. If the primary motivation is self-protection or protection from liability, the communication will not be direct. To stay authentic and trustworthy, educators need to say what they mean and mean what they say. If we are caught in a cycle of fear, where we are afraid to speak the truth, there is no clarity or trust.

Likewise, private meetings excluding parents where the "real" discussion takes place is another way to miss opportunities for authenticity and to hide what's really going on. If there is something that needs to be said in private and not in front of a parent, consider why that is the case. What is being held back? What is gained by sharing the truth outside the parents' awareness? What may be the downside?

Building the skills to be compassionate and direct can ease the drain that comes with difficult conversations. We don't need to make promises or have the answers. We can show genuine concern, think collaboratively and open-mindedly, resist rushing to judgment and stay observant, and be honest, even when it's uncomfortable. This authenticity goes much further than a false sense of knowing, a plan of action that is unclear, or passing the buck.

## A School Culture of Co-Regulation and Personal Accountability

When we prioritize and support personal development, we naturally enhance the relationships across the system. We create a culture of safety, which optimizes learning and growth. The relationship focused, openness, and curiosity become a way of being in the school. The culture supports this reflective work, recognizes our common humanity, and fosters compassion. These resilient qualities and characteristics are modeled and experienced across the system. This way of being sustains with turnover, because it is not dependent on a specific program and is infused throughout the culture.

Part III provides practices to become more self-aware of body and mind and to deepen connection with others. These skills can be practiced individually, in pairs, or in small or large groups. The only tools needed are paper and a writing instrument or a notetaking device, the motivation to enhance well-being, and an open mind to grow, personally and professionally.

# PART III

*Practices to Resource the Educator*

## Bottom-Up Practices

The state of our physical body influences our interpretation of emotion and cues others to our emotional state. Sensations, muscle tension or relaxation, tone of voice, facial expression, and body posture influence our perception of our emotional state and communicate the state to others. With awareness, we can shift the body to shift our state and communicate something different to ourselves and others.

Interoception is the perception of sensations from inside the body and includes the perception of physical sensations related to internal organ functions, such as heart rate, respiration, and satiety.[1] People vary in how tuned in they are to the inner workings of the body. We can become better at noticing the fluctuations of the internal body experience through practice.

One of the benefits of formal interoceptive practices, such as body scans or mindful movement, is that we strengthen our ability to notice subtle shifts in our physical state. The more cued in we are to our physical state, the more conscious control we have over it.

Informal interoceptive practices involve quick check-ins, in the moment. While we can pause and tap into our physical experience at any time, a regular, formal practice builds interoceptive skill and makes the informal practices more accessible. Regular practice increases the likelihood that we will call on it in the moment, rather than fall into old patterns. What follows are both formal and informal body-based practices.

## Working with Posture

Postural shifts, including full body postures, gestures, and facial expression influence our physiology.[2] Gestures and postures have arisen in our collective consciousness and can be seen represented across the world in various cultures, rituals, and belief systems. They likely reflect what has been experienced.

### Signaling Safety

**Purpose:** to position the body such that it cues the nervous system for safety.

To send a signal of safety to the nervous system, sit up straight, lengthen the spine, or stand tall. Open through the chest and relax the shoulders, such that they fall away from the ears. Arms may rest gently at sides or hands rest on thighs, if sitting.

Throughout the day, notice when you are contracted or collapsed through the chest or tensing the abdomen. Gently shift into this posture to signal calm to the body.

This posture frees up the diaphragm, allowing the lungs to expand more fully. Try breathing more deeply, expanding through the belly. Holding this posture is incompatible with anxiety. This position cues the nervous system that all is safe and well.

## Safe Boundary

**Purpose:** to protect oneself energetically from receiving negativity.

Though an open posture is a relaxed posture, there are times when protecting ourselves is wise.

When feeling the need for a physical boundary or for protection, energetically wrap your arms around the front body (belly) as if protecting your organs. This gesture is self-protective and self-compassionate.

After the threat is no longer detected, try moving back to an open, relaxed posture.

## Balancing Openness and Protection

Adapted from Omega Institute cofounder Elizabeth Lesser, *Broken Open: How Difficult Times Can Help Us Grow*.[3] These gestures are found in many traditions.

**Purpose:** to embody the physiology of holding a boundary while remaining open to others. To explore how embodying the meaning of the gesture influences the mind.

Described below are two separate gestures, typically used together for balance.

### *Abhaya Mudra*

Hold the right hand at shoulder height, the arm crooked, with palm facing outward, fingers upright and joined, in a stop position.

This mudra symbolizes protection or the holding of a boundary. It is the embodiment of "no."

> While holding the gesture, notice how it feels to hold a strong boundary. Does it feel natural or unnatural? Note any thoughts, sensations, emotions, or images that arise.
>
> Release the gesture. Write about your experience or discuss with a partner.

### Verada Mudra

With the left hand, hold your cupped hand palm up in front of you in a receiving gesture. This gesture is useful when wanting to be open to the voices and experiences of others.

While holding the gesture, notice how it feels to be open to receiving or to open yourself up to others. Note any thoughts, sensations, emotions, or images that arise.

Release the gesture. Write about your experience or discuss with a partner.

Now, try balancing openness with self-protection by holding both gestures, at once. Notice any thoughts, sensations, emotions, or images that arise. Share the experience as you are willing.

Often, we are more able to give and be accepting of others when we balance having boundaries but remain open to others.

## Root to Rise

**Purpose:** to create stability and expansion in the body and mind.

This can be practiced standing, seated in a chair, or seated on the floor.

Plant your feet firmly on the ground. Shifting the weight, from toes to heel, and outer to inner edges of the feet, find balance in the distribution of weight. Feel the sturdiness of your legs. As you breathe deeply into the belly, visualize roots reaching down from the feet deep into the earth.

Imagine the body rising up out of the feet and pelvis. Lengthen the spine to draw the crown of the head toward the sky.

Breathe deeply as you notice the opposition of reaching down and rising up.

**Seated Variation:** Sitting in a sturdy chair, place feet on the floor. Shift hips forward and back, side to side in the chair. Notice the support of the chair beneath you and the soles of the feet on the ground. Lengthen the spine, open the chest, drop the shoulders, and visualize the crown of the head moving toward the sky.

This posture is useful when feeling ungrounded and is an effective way to begin any of the reflective cognitive exercises.

## Roll with the Punches

**Purpose:** to practice being nonresistant and bending so not to break.

In martial arts and boxing, physics is used to an advantage. Instead of meeting incoming force with resistance, there is fluid movement away from the force, thereby meeting it with empty space.

We have a tendency to contract and resist to brace against pain or discomfort. Rather than reflexively tensing or pushing back, we can choose to relax into it and stay flexible by relaxing into the tension or breathing into the held breath.

In practice, when you feel resistance of mind or body against an incoming threat, imagine the force slipping by or rolling off the body as you stay flexible and relaxed. Notice the restriction of breath and deliberately exhale completely and then inhale slowly and deeply, soften the belly. Notice any contraction of musculature and deliberately release the contraction.

## Posture of Compassion

**Purpose:** to keep our mind and heart open and encourage compassion.

Notice any contraction through the front body. Lift shoulders toward ears and allow them to relax.

Take in a deep breath and imagine an expansion in the chest as your heart is free to float up and out.

The posture is similar to "Signaling Safety," but with the intention of sending compassion to another. We cannot be compassionate without feeling safe.

## Embodying Courage

**Purpose:** to produce a posture that signals fearlessness or courage in the face of fear.

A variation of a power pose.[4]

To embody the pose, stand with feet shoulder-width or wider apart. Place fists on hips as you lift the chest and pull back the shoulders to open through the chest. Chin and gaze may lift upward as comfortable. This looks like the Wonder Woman stance.

This pose is useful as a practice to shift out of doubt, fear, or trepidation and embody confidence.

# Heart Opening

**Purpose:** a formal practice to change the shape and patterning of the body, to counteract the collapsed tendency of everyday living, and to shift emotional experience.

This supported pose creates a passive stretch to release through the front body and to deepen the breath. Passive stretching allows for resistant patterns in the body to release. This restorative pose can be accomplished with everyday props, such as towels or small blankets if bolsters are not available.

To support and provide lift under the back, fold a soft blanket or a towel three to four inches in thickness. Position yourself to sit directly in front of the blanket, with the edge of the blanket at your sacrum. Lie back slowly with your spine fully supported. If your head comes off the top, place a folded towel or a light pillow under your head. You may want a small rolled-up towel to support the neck and maintain the natural curve of the neck.

Place a larger rolled-up towel of desired height under the knees to maintain the natural lumbar curve in the low back. Allow the arms to fall to the sides of the body.

The goal is to provide a gentle, passive opening across the chest and the abdomen. This gentle release is key for the nervous to be able to settle. Remain in this position for five to ten minutes or as long as comfortable.

Practicing this formal postural shift can release chronically held patterns and makes other postures, such as "Signaling Safety," "Posture of Compassion," and" Embodying Courage," more accessible.

# Letting Go

**Purpose:** to release held tension throughout the back, body, and head and to release any mental stressors weighing on you.

**Contraindications:** avoid the posture if you have untreated high blood pressure, low blood pressure, or glaucoma.

Start in a standing position. With a bend in the knees, so as not to strain the hamstrings or lower back, drop the chin toward the chest and gently round your back, lowering your head toward the floor. You may have slightly bent knees or significantly bent knees, depending on what is best for your body and the level of tension you'd like to produce. A deeper bend in the knees will release the spine rather than the hamstrings.

Let the arms fall toward the floor and relax through the shoulders. Allow the weight of the head to provide a gentle stretch of the back. Release the jaw and tongue, and let gravity do the work.

Stay in this position from ten to ninety seconds, or as long as it feels good and productive. Move slowly and carefully, unrolling back into standing, so as not to be dizzy from less blood flow to the head.

**Seated Variation:** If a standing position is not accessible or recommended (see contraindications above), a variation is to sit in a sturdy chair and gently fold forward, using a pillow on your thighs to rest on, if desired.

On a physiological level, allowing your head to gently put traction on the spine creates more space between the vertebrae and allows the cerebral spinal fluid to flow more easily. The muscles along the spine, which work hard to keep us upright and can become stuck in tension patterns, have an opportunity to relax, and blood flows to the head, bringing increased oxygen. It offers a relaxing of the tongue and jaw, which is difficult to do in an upright position.

Metaphorically, we can envision letting go of the thoughts, beliefs, emotions, grudges, or worries that we hold. Imagine the thoughts, negative emotions, or heaviness pouring out through the head into the ground.

Physically and metaphorically, we can use this for a change in perspective to see things from a different vantage point.

## Constructive Rest

**Purpose:** to position the body such that the large muscles activated in the stress response can completely relax. To create a feedback loop of safety and relaxation.

When the body is in a state of contraction, particularly the quadriceps and hip flexors, it can signal the brain into fight or flight. These large muscles are mobilized during sympathetic activation as a means to run or fight. Everyday demands, such as sitting for long periods of time, shorten the hip flexors, and they can become chronically shortened or contracted. When in this shortened or tight state, this positioning signals the nervous system for sympathetic activation, even if no threat exists.

Actively stretching the hip flexors (quadriceps and iliopsoas) can be counterproductive as the force may create more contraction, initially. Instead, positioning the body such that these structures are allowed to completely relax shifts the body out of fight or flight. That is, allow the hip flexors to relax by putting them in a neutral position with no demand on them.

To achieve this deep relaxation, do the following exercise.

Lie on the floor, placing a blanket underneath the lower

back for comfort, if desired. Rest your calves over a chair, bed, couch, or other stable object, so that your hips are at ninety degrees (thighs to abdomen) and knees are at ninety degrees (thighs to calves). Legs should feel stable to fully relax.

What is most important is that the hip flexors can completely let go and are not under any tension while holding the legs up. Settle in for fifteen to twenty minutes and breathe slowly and deeply, if possible. After the release, you may want to gently stretch the hip flexors if it feels good to do so, as they will be more likely to release.

# Eye Movement

Our eyes hold somatic memory and have habitual patterns of tension and movement based on emotion and experience. The contraction of the muscles around the eyes are used to communicate threat or safety to others.[5] We can release tension and activate the brain through eye movement.

## Widening the Eyes to Wonder

**Purpose:** to change perspective and shift into curiosity

We tend to focus and narrow our vision when under stress. This unconscious process is adaptive to focus our attention on the threat, but not always useful. We can open our eyes wide (wonder) to interrupt the stress response and become open to curiosity.

In a stressful encounter, to counter the hyper-focusing tendency and change perspective, deliberately widen the eyes by opening widely and raising the eyebrows.

## Infinity Eye Tracing

**Purpose:** to release tension throughout the body. To activate the right and left hemispheres of the brain.

Holding the head in a neutral position and shifting the gaze right and left without moving the head, you may notice soreness or tenderness around the eyes. It may be more intense in one direction than another. The strain in the eyes transmits to the rest of the body. Relaxing the eyes by changing the point of focus, moving in all directions, can release tension throughout the body.

Imagine a sideways figure eight or an infinity symbol in front of the eyes. Trace the image with only the eyes, keeping the head steady. Without moving the head, look up and to the right, trace the eyes down and to the right, then diagonally up and to the left, down and to the left. Continue tracing the figure eight. This activates all parts of the brain while releasing tension in the eyes and its connecting structures.

This can be practiced with eyes opened or closed.

Whenever we cross the midline of our bodies or alternate stimulating the right and left sides of the body, we are integrating across the left and right brain hemispheres.

## Body Scan

Adapted from UCLA Mindful Awareness Research Center.[6]

**Purpose:** to practice tuning into body sensations, being with it, noticing, and staying curious. To practice the skill of interoception.

Research shows that you cannot experience your body and think self-referentially about your body at the same time. Different parts of the brain are activated. Practicing experiencing the body strengthens connections in the part of the brain that deactivate self-conscious and self-referential parts, associated with negative emotion.

This can be a formal practice, taking your time, or an informal practice, moving more quickly through the body.

The body scan can be performed while lying down, sitting, or in other postures.

This script is best read by someone in the room or pre-recorded as audio.

>Begin by bringing your attention to your body.

>If it is comfortable for you, close your eyes or lower your eyes and gaze softly at the floor.

>Notice your body, wherever you're seated. Feel the weight of your body on the chair, on the floor. (pause)

Inhale gently and deeply, releasing the breath at your own pace. (pause)

As you breathe in, envision oxygenated blood circulating throughout the body. As you exhale, let go of tension to relax more deeply.

Notice your feet on the floor. Notice the sensations of the soles of your feet touching the floor. The weight, pressure, vibration, heat. (pause)

Notice your legs against the chair. The pressure, pulsing, heaviness, lightness. (pause)

Notice your back against the chair. (pause)

Bring your attention to your stomach area. If your stomach is tense or tight, let it soften. Take a breath. (pause)

Become aware of your hands. Notice any sensations in your hands. Allow them to soften. (pause)

Notice your arms. Feel any sensations in your arms. Let your shoulders be soft. (pause)

Notice your neck and throat. Let them be soft. Relax. (pause)

Soften your jaw. Let your face and facial muscles be soft. (pause)

You may take inventory of your entire body from feet to head.

Notice any remaining tension and let it go.
Take one more breath.

When you're ready, open your eyes and reorient to the room.

## Grounding through the Senses

**Purpose:** to come back into the body when stress or a trigger pulls you out of the body. To ground the body through attention to the senses.

Activate the senses to keep you in the present, rather than being pulled out of the moment by a memory or into the future with anxiety.

When feeling overwhelmed, anxious, or scattered, notice one aspect in the environment that you can see, hear, taste, smell, or feel. This open awareness brings us back to the present moment, out of the analytical brain and into the sensing body.

Touch can be especially grounding. You may notice the sensation of your feet on the ground or your hips in a seat. Holding an object and bringing attention to the weight or texture can be useful as a point of focus.

This informal practice is useful for coming into the present moment. For instance, if we find our minds are worrying or anticipating the future, or regretting, ruminating about the past, we can halt the thought stream by conscious awareness of sensations in the present.

# Conscious Breathing

It is estimated that we take about 17,000 breaths a day. Most of this is done without conscious awareness. Manipulating the breath is one of the most powerful ways to influence our physiology.[7] Below are a variety of ways to work with the breath for desired outcomes.

Breath practices can be done formally as part of other meditative or reflective practices, or informally in the moment when we notice and desire a shift in physiology.

## Lengthen the Exhale

**Purpose:** to shift into parasympathetic dominance and interrupt sympathetic nervous system activation by sending signals to the brain to calm.

When we exhale, we turn on vagal inhibition to the heart, slowing heart rate and lowering blood pressure. As we inhale, this inhibition is turned off, thereby allowing the heart rate to increase.

We often are breathing shallow and in the upper part of the chest. Breathing this way activates the sympathetic nervous system and mobilizes the body. This can be experienced as anxiety.

When we breathe slowly and deeply, softening the belly and encouraging the diaphragm to contract and drop down, we expand the lungs more fully.

The vagus nerve is a long wandering nerve that begins in the brainstem and wanders to the face and head, down through the chest cavity and through the diaphragm into the organs below the diaphragm. This nerve allows for communication between the organs and the brain in both directions. When we deepen our breath, activating the diaphragm, and slow the release of the breath, we signal the brain, via the vagus nerve, that all is well, and we are safe.

**Practice**

Breathe slowly through the nose, relaxing the belly and fully expanding through the belly and chest. Exhale slowly, taking more time to exhale than to inhale. For instance, breathe into a count of four and exhale to a count of six. Some people find it useful to imagine releasing the breath through an imaginary straw to slow the release. After a few rounds of in and out breaths, the body moves out of sympathetic dominance (activation/fight/flight) and into parasympathetic dominance (rest and digest).

## Energetic Breath (Bellows Breath)

**Purpose:** to activate the sympathetic nervous system via the breath, bringing energy and mobilization to the body.

When we take a big breath with a quick forceful exhale, we signal the brain via the vagus nerve to activate and mobilize. Vagal inhibition is released, and the heart rate increases, pumping oxygenated blook quickly though the body, waking us up, becoming more alert.

An energetic breath is useful when feeling sluggish or tired, such as midafternoon slump, or getting psyched for physical activity. Be careful if prone to anxiety when using bellows breath, as this can trigger panic or intense anxiety as it activates the sympathetic nervous system.

### Practice

Inhale deeply and exhale quickly and forcefully, all at once or in several short bursts until emptying the lungs.

> **Note:** Moving too far and quickly from the current rate of breathing can be disruptive. Instead, match the current breath and slowly transition to the desired rate and ratio of inhale to exhale.

## Coherence Breathing

**Purpose:** to increase heart rate variability, which is an indicator of a flexible and responsive nervous system.[8]

Our natural tendency is to breathe at a rate of two to three seconds per inhale and exhale. We also have a tendency to breathe high in the chest and not engage the diaphragm fully.

An optimal cadence of breath is five to six breaths per minute or five to six seconds in and five to six seconds out.

**Practice**

Three minutes a day, when possible.

Focus on breathing diaphragmatically. Breathing in and out through the nose, gently place a hand on your belly to encourage the relaxation and expansion of the belly to facilitate the downward contraction of the diaphragm.

## Heart-Focused Breathing
Adapted from HeartMath Institute.[9]

**Purpose:** to connect to the physiology of compassion. Useful when preparing for a difficult encounter.

With eyes open, softly gazing, or eyes closed, notice that you are breathing. And notice the natural quality of expansion and when you breathe out that expansion dissolves. Let yourself receive the breath and then release the breath.

You may place a hand over the heart/chest, and as you breathe, see if you can feel the expansion around the heart as you breathe in.

With hands on your lap or by your side, imagine breathing directly into the heart area and breathing a little more deeply than normal. As you breathe in, imagine the flow of air entering directly into the heart through the chest wall and leaving from the heart on the exhale. Visualize the energy flowing into the heart.

Imagine any strength, courage, or kindness you need, that you can breathe it into your own heart.

This can be practiced at any time, but especially when you feel a stressful encounter or racing thoughts.

Drawn-on breath is strengthening and nourishing and can connect you to something bigger than self—faith, community that cares, ancestors, force of life—through the breath. Drawing on the breath as a resource that is linked to imagery can stabilize the nervous system and activate the physiology of compassion.

This practice is useful for creating stability in the face of suffering. Choose to connect to the positive motivation of love and care by imaging this breath as a vehicle for love, support, or courage. It activates systems of your brain and body that give you a felt sense of love and hope.

## Breathing Alters Perception

**Purpose:** to notice how breathing affects our emotions, our cognition, and our perceptions of others.

In pairs, decide which partner will manipulate breath and which partner will observe.

For the person manipulating the breath, start by breathing with long inhalations, short exhalations.

☞ Ask what the person manipulating the breathing noticed about themselves. What thoughts, emotions, or sensations arise? How does the person manipulating the breath perceive the partner?

☞ The observer is asked to note what they experience internally and how they perceive the partner.

**Reverse the Physiology**

Person manipulating breath now breathes in normally and extends the exhale.

☞ Ask what the person manipulating the breathing noticed about themselves. What thoughts, emotions, or sensations arise?

☞ How does the person manipulating the breath perceive the partner?

☞ The observer is asked to note what they experience internally and how they perceive the partner.

It is not uncommon for the person shortening the exhale to feel like they've done something wrong or to perceive their partner as being judgmental. The internal sensations brought on by activating the stress response influences our perceptions. They detect threat instead of safety.

When the physiology is reversed, and the manipulator extends the exhale (thereby switching to parasympathetic), they perceive their partner as attractive and likeable. They detect safety instead of threat.

# Sound/Vibration

Vocalizations, humming, and singing help to shift the nervous system from a sympathetic-dominant (fight/flight) to a parasympathetic-dominant (rest/digest) state. Mechanisms involved may include increased afferent signaling from the diaphragm due to stretching by prolonged exhalation, increased visceral afferent impulses from the abdomen due to sound vibration, and resetting the breathing to a more parasympathetic pattern by lessening carbon dioxide loss by slowing the breath rhythm and extending the exhalation. The deep pitch of the sound may also play a role.[10]

## Bumblebee Breath (Bhramari Pranayama)

**Purpose:** to relieve stress, agitation or anger through a soothing breath and vibration. To calm the body and mind.

Find a comfortable seated position.

As you settle into your seat, close your eyes or lower your gaze. Notice the feeling of the ground, cushion, or chair beneath you, and energetically ground down through your hipbones while lengthening through a long spine.

Breathe in and out through your nose. Relax your face and jaw, keeping the lips gently closed, while allowing your teeth to remain separated.

Gently press your pointer fingers on the cartilage of your ears just below your cheekbones, blocking any external sound.

Keeping your ears blocked, take a deep breath in through your nose and exhale through your nose. On your exhale, make a humming or buzzing sound.

Continue for at least six cycles of breath, or as long as you like.

After completing Bhramari breathing, take a few moments to sit in silence and allow yourself to breathe naturally.

## Sounding

Adapted from medical biophysicist and psychologist Peter A. Levine, *In an Unspoken Voice: How the Body Releases Trauma and Restores Goodness.*[11]

**Purpose:** to create vibration in the belly to interrupt the freeze response and signal the nervous system to calm.

Take in an easy full breath, and on the exhalation, make the sound "voo" as if it's coming from the gut or the viscera.

As you sound, you'll notice where you feel the vibration and play with it until you can sense it in the belly. After the full exhale, take a natural inhale and repeat. Repeat as many times as feels useful.

## Singing

**Purpose:** to create vagal inhibition by naturally lengthening the exhale while singing. To experience the joy of singing.

Singing is a way to connect to joy, to express oneself, to connect with others, and to have fun. One physiological bonus to singing is that it naturally lengthens the exhale, thereby shifting us into parasympathetic dominance.

Singing to and with your class can bring everyone into a calmer, more socially connected state.

## Mind/Body Reading

**Purpose:** to practice "reading" others' internal states through nonverbal cues. To notice how the thoughts and emotions held by others is mirrored in our bodies and informs our understanding of others' internal states.

This exercise is practiced in pairs.

Decide who will be observed and who will be the observer.

Partner A (the observed) brings to mind an event associated with a strong emotion. Do not disclose any details of the experience. Instead, mentally recall the emotional experience. After a few minutes, pause and write what comes up in your internal experience (thoughts, emotions, body sensations).

Partner B (the observer) quietly observes the nonverbal signals of Partner A. Note any thoughts, sensations, or images that arise in yourself. Pause and write what you are feeling and sensing in yourself as you observed Partner A.

When finished, compare notes about what each is thinking, feeling, sensing, or detecting. Discuss the ways in which the perceptions aligned and where they differed.

If desired, partners can switch roles and repeat.

This illustrates how our conscious and unconscious detection of others' nonverbal cues is mirrored in our bodies. As we detect the cues in our own bodies, we interpret them based on our histories, filtering or distorting aspects. In this way, we sense another's internal experience by feeling it in our bodies, but may misinterpret the cues.

## Sense and Savor

**Purpose:** to counteract the default mode of the brain. To practice noticing and amplifying positive sensation or experience.

Our brains have a tendency to ruminate and amplify the negative but not the positive. We are also often thinking about the past or the future, rather than the current moment. We can bring balance back to our experiences by deliberately noticing and staying with the positive experience. Anytime we experience a pleasurable emotion or sensation, we can stay with it and amplify it, rather than rushing on to the next thing.

When you find something delightful or pleasant, focus your attention on the subtle aspects of the moment. Tune into the pleasant feelings, sensations, or attributes of the event. Focus attention on the pleasurable sensations to amplify the good feelings.

You can set an intention to savor a particular experience, such as focusing on the sight, smell, and taste of a nice meal, or by taking yourself on a sense and savor walk, noticing the beauty of nature, the sun on your body, the smell of fresh air.

This can also be an informal practice where we stumble upon a beautiful scene or experience throughout the day, and we stop to really notice and experience it. Or by bringing our attention to the pleasant sensation of an everyday task, such as fully appreciating the hot water pelting your body in the shower.

## Embodied Reward

**Purpose:** to associate a better-feeling body with less judgment. To "teach" or encourage our body to stay out of judgment by reaping the rewards.

The next time you catch yourself in a place of judgment and are able to shift to curiosity, notice what it feels like in your body.

What is the sensation of judgment?

How does it feel to stay out of judgment?

Notice less tension, easier breath, more expansion, less contraction.

If you find you are not able to shift out of judgment, notice what that feels like in the body. Describe the sensations. Locate any sensations in the body and bring attention to them. Breathe into it. Notice if the sensations intensify or dissipate.

## Resourcing through Nature

**Purpose:** to self-regulate and replenish through exposure to nature.

Research supports the positive mental and the physical effects of being in or around nature. For instance, being in nature reduces rumination.[12] Window views that include natural elements (compared with window views that do not) are associated with superior memory, attention, and impulse inhibition[13] as well as greater feelings of well-being and positive mood.[14] When being in nature is not accessible, bringing plants into the classroom can serve the same purpose. Even artwork or photographs of nature scenes have a calming and rejuvenating effect on those taking it in.[15]

To reap the regulating effects of nature, make time to be outdoors, in a natural environment, when possible. When not possible, look out at nature or bring nature into the classroom with live plants or through sounds and images.

Practicing open awareness or sense and savor may amplify the experience and benefits.

## Top-Down Exercises

Cognition affects regulation. Our thoughts, beliefs, assumptions, expectations, and mindsets influence our experience by filtering information and interpretation. Our thoughts are both affected by our physiology and influence our physiology.

Using reflective exercises to become aware of and change our thinking can be an effective means toward self-regulation and well-being. When higher-level thinking and problem-solving are not accessible, as in moments of overwhelming stress, bottom-up practices can bring us back into regulation allowing for the top-down reflective work. What follows are a number of cognitive practices to enhance well-being, improve relationships, and keep us in wonder.

## Power of Expectations

**Purpose:** to get curious about how we may be influencing another's behavior with our expectations. To challenge our expectations.

Bring to mind a favorite student. You may recall a specific interaction or a general sense of the relationship.

Note the thoughts that come to mind.

Consider what you expect from this student academically.

Consider what you expect from this student behaviorally.

Tune into your body.

Describe any sensations or the relative ease/unease in your body. Take a moment to write down what arises.

Now, consider how this student perceives you. How might he/she feel with and about you? Pause and write.

Now, consider a challenging student or relationship.

You may recall a specific interaction or a general sense of the relationship.

Note any thoughts come to mind.

Consider what you expect from this student academically.

Consider what you expect from this student behaviorally.

Tune into your body.

Describe any sensations or the relative ease/unease in your body. Take a moment to write down what arises.

Take note of any discrepancies in mind/body when considering the two relationships.

Consider how a positive expectation might shift your behavior or feelings toward the person. Pause and write.

Consider how shifting what you expect from the person influences their perception of themselves or experiences with you. Pause and write.

If working in pairs or a group, share your experience, as comfortable.

## Impact of Language

**Purpose:** to notice how a shift in language changes how we perceive another person.

Bring a student to mind. Generate five to ten descriptive words or phrases that come to mind when you think of this student.

Pause and write down the descriptors.

Notice the quality of the descriptors. Are most positive, negative, or a mix? Are they objective or interpretations? Notice how the negative words feel in your body as you use them. Note any sensations that arise in your body.

Are there positive or neutral words you could accurately use to describe the person. If so, rewrite the description using the neutral or positive words. Notice how it feels to write positive descriptors.

Consider how word choice may subtly shift how you experience this person. How does your view of them affect your behavior in relation to them?

Set the intention to notice the language in thought and speech that you use with/about this person. When catching the negative descriptors, try speaking and thinking with neutral or positive descriptors instead. Stay curious about how this shifts the relationship.

## Setting an Intention

**Purpose:** to make a small, effortless, intentional change to effect big change over time.

It is the small but consistent behaviors that effect the most change.

Consider how a challenging student experiences you. (See "Power of Expectations" exercise.)

Consider a behavioral change or way of thinking about a student that might shift the way a student perceives you or perceives himself or herself.

Set yourself up as a key participant in shifting the trajectory for this student, simply by shifting a minor interaction over time.

Be specific. What does this look like? Is it a verbal interaction, a nonverbal interaction, or a way of thinking or speaking about the student? For instance, you may greet the student differently, pay closer attention to your body language when interacting, become aware of your facial expressions, choose different language when communicating, be nonreactive to difficult behavior, or ask about his or her day.

Set an intention to have a different experience with this

student. A small shift in the daily experience of this student could set a new trajectory.

Commit to being this way daily for a week, a month, or longer. It's the day-to-day and moment-to-moment interactions that make the most impact. After a week or more, reflect on if and how the energy and transaction has shifted the relationship.

These small changes can affect the relationship and affect how the student and educator see themselves. Positive changes carry through to other relationships and can affect a student for years to come. Having a different relationship with you changes what is possible in all relationships and carries into the future.

Notice when your behavior falls short of the intention. Be curious and kind to yourself about why this might be. Every moment is a new moment. You can always begin again.

## Redemption Story

**Purpose:** to change the narrative about a struggling student, thereby shifting expectations.

Beliefs about self and others infuse into everything we do. When we lower expectations because of a belief—such as a student being disadvantaged due to trauma, poverty, or an unfair start to life—we can unconsciously add to the problem with our contaminating expectations.

This exercise can be completed alone or shared with a partner.

Educators may feel the burden of playing the role of savoir for a student, and this can overwhelm. We don't need to fix circumstances to have a positive influence. Our redemption beliefs influence the student, both consciously and unconsciously.

Rewrite the story for your most challenging student, rising above the challenge or growing because of the challenge.

How might their setbacks inspire them? What strengths have been exhibited in the struggle? How might these skills serve them now and in the future?

Include aspects of agency, lessons learned, and resilience.

Consider the role you play in changing the trajectory of this student. How might making a small shift in your relationship affect big change over time? (See "Setting an Intention" exercise.)

Project their trajectory one to five years into the future. How may these changes in how you view the student and/or how they view themselves affect their relationships, choices, and academic achievements?

After writing the Redemption Story, share with a partner, if desired.

## Observation vs. Evaluation

Adapted from psychologist Marshall Rosenberg, *Nonviolent Communication: A Language of Life: Life-Changing Tools for Healthy Relationships.*[16]

**Purpose:** to challenge assumptions and wonder about behavior. To discern between observable behavior and interpretation.

An *observation* is a statement about behavior that can be directly observed: The student is slumped over his desk.

An *evaluation* is an interpretation of an observable behavior: The student is bored. The student is lazy.

In the evaluation statement, we have made an assumption or jumped to a conclusion. While we may be correct, our interpretations are influenced by past experience, expectation, and our state of mind at the time of the observation, and therefore open to error. We can practice sticking with the raw data of observation.

**Practice**

Bring to mind a student who engaged in an undesirable behavior. Pause and write about the behavior. Consider whether the description is observable fact or evaluation/interpretation.

❦ If you find you are making an interpretation, return to the observable behaviors that led to this conclusion. (That is, my student doesn't complete her work or turn it in on time.) This is the observation.

❦ Ask yourself, what other possible explanations can there be for this behavior?

To practice in the moment, the next time you are making an assessment about a student or creating a story about a student's behavior, pause and ask yourself, "Is this observation or evaluation? Have I moved from the objective to the subjective?" If an assumption has been made, consider other possible explanations for the behavior or observation, especially if the initial assumption was negative.

Taking note of the observable behavior, you may also reflect on the behavior during a less stressful time. When we are less stressed and more clear-headed, we are open to multiple explanations.

## Identifying Triggers

**Purpose:** to notice patterns in our reactivity. To draw on multiple interactions, experiences, or relationships to find common thread or triggers.

Our tendencies will reveal themselves if we look with compassion and curiosity at our behavior across relationships.

Think of three or more people in your life with whom you've had challenging interactions or negative emotions.

Is there something in common about how you perceive them, how you feel with them? With kindness, consider that there is a button, a wound, or a trigger in you that is being activated in each scenario. Sometimes we know (or we think we know) the root of this trigger. Often, we do not. It's not necessary to know the root.

We can become aware of our tendency and look at it with kindness or even humor when we see it arise. We create space when we see it for what it is, a tendency to react with a specific emotion or behavior. We can name it and thereby externalize it so that it is something that happens to us, and is not us. Every person we interact with is a mirror in that way. The people who challenge us the most are our greatest teachers.

Which behaviors in others push your buttons the most? Consider why this might be.

Reflect on three interactions from separate people where you felt a similar sensation, emotion, or negative thoughts about yourself or the person.

Get back to the raw data. What specifically pushed your button? Tone of voice, body language, word choice, perception of their intention, negative emotion toward you, assuming a motivation?

Knowing our triggers is empowering. It allows us to hold that feeling with compassion without impulsively reacting, so that we can choose to respond in a way that serves us and the relationship.

## The Space Between

Adapted from embodiment expert Wendy Palmer and neuroscientist Janet Crawford, *Leadership Embodiment: How the Way We Sit and Stand Can Change the Way We Think and Speak.*[17]

**Purpose:** to practice holding another's difficult behavior toward us without reactivity. To use visualization to create space between others' reactivity and our own. To practice not taking other peoples' behavior personally and staying present in the communication.

Other people's behavior is not about us. As humans, it is natural to take anger, disrespect, blame, and other negative expressions toward us personally.

In a moment of difficult interaction, we can also use a visualization to protect against the unwanted negativity and stay open to the communication.

Create a space to "catch" the negativity.

> Imagine a receptacle between you and the other person. Create this in any way that comes to mind. It may be a box, a barrel, a bucket, or any other container that comes to mind. Imagine the words and energy coming from the other person landing in the container. It is held there where you can see it for what it is

(pain emanating from the other person). Stay curious or move away.

If you want to take the visualization further, you can visualize the receptacle transforming the negative energy into love and acceptance and send it back to the person or to yourself.

## Iceberg of Needs

**Purpose:** to practice mentalizing or understanding another's inner world. To wonder about what lies beneath behavior. To get to the root cause of behavior.

Behavior is a response to emotions and needs. The behaviors are what is observable. The emotions are just under the surface and may be easily seen, though may not tell the whole story. Deeper, still, are unmet needs.

When we stay curious about needs, we have a better chance of getting to the root problem and have some direction about acknowledging and, when possible, meeting needs, both of which help to regulate emotion. From there, undesirable behavior may fall away. The image of an iceberg captures what is seen and unseen.

Reflect on an interaction or experience that was challenging. Consider the undesirable behavior in another person and your reactivity to it. Or, perhaps an action you took that was not in your best interest.

Draw an image of an iceberg tip out of the water, with the bulk of the iceberg hidden below the water line. On the tip of the iceberg, write down the behavior (something that was said or done) that was difficult. Try not to make any interpretations, simply describe the behavior.

Under the water line, list the possible emotions this person was feeling when he or she engaged in the behavior.

Next, deeper down in the iceberg, write the unmet needs that may explain the emotion. Recognize that we all have needs that go unmet and can cause great distress, resulting in unwanted behavior. Bring compassion to the person, especially if that person is you.

It may be useful to refer to the list of behaviors/emotions/needs on the following chart. This list is not exhaustive, nor does one behavior result from any one emotion. Any behavior can spring from any overwhelming emotion. It's helpful to consider the list when we catch ourselves jumping to negative assumptions about a person's behavior.

Educators have found it useful to use the emotions and needs columns of the list with students to normalize the range of needs and emotions and to more easily identify what they are feeling and needing.

| Behaviors | Emotions | Needs |
| --- | --- | --- |
| hitting | angry | food |
| swearing | annoyed | water |
| pushing | confused | rest |
| biting | disappointed | movement |
| grabbing | discouraged | acceptance |
| zoning out | distressed | connection |
| fidgeting | embarrassed | physical safety |
| controlling | anxious | emotional safety |
| withdrawing | frustrated | compassion |
| hiding | helpless | respect |
| crying | hopeless | trust |
| whining | humiliated | understanding |
| fleeing | impatient | appreciation |
| clinging | irritated | love |
| bullying | lonely | reassurance |
| sarcastic | misunderstood | creativity |
| demanding | abandoned | inspiration |
| blaming | overwhelmed | authenticity |
| inflexible | scared | fun/play |
| destructive | sad | freedom |
| shutting down | ashamed | contribution |

©2016 Witness and Wonder

## Drop the Story

**Purpose:** to tune into emotion and sensation without layering on an interpretation or narrative. To notice our tendency to create a narrative to account for sensation and emotion.

Think of a moderately emotional event or experience.

With a partner, tell what happened by only talking about feelings and sensations, giving no details of the actual events or context. Give no explanation for why you felt what you did.

Note what it felt like to stay with only the emotional content without revealing the narrative.

Switch roles with your partner and repeat.

Share your experience of the exercise with each other and/or with a larger group.

## Make the Implicit Explicit

**Purpose:** to clarify and make obvious your internal experience (thoughts, motivations, feelings) that is driving behavior. To make explicit the relationship between internal experience and behavior.

Some students will have trouble reading emotions and nonverbal cues. They may miss or misread cues, both intentional and unintentional. We can foster social and emotional development when we speak aloud what's driving our behavior, putting words to feelings, and talking about needs. This is especially useful when we are experiencing negative emotion that may be conveyed in our bodies. In this way, we connect thoughts and feelings to behavior.

This is a useful practice for repair when there has been a rupture in the relationship. When we repair, especially with younger children, we can talk about what we were thinking and feeling and how those thoughts and feelings influenced our behavior. Then, we talk about the steps we took to bring ourselves back to regulation and what that feels like.

Speaking about internal experiences normalizes the range of human emotion and needs. It brings awareness to the internal experience, rather than the event or action that is observable.

**Practice**

I am feeling _____ because _____.

(Describe the thoughts or needs driving the emotion.)

Next, decide to model, explicitly, the action taken to regain equilibrium.

I'm going to_____ (take a breath/move my body, focus my attention/talk to someone I trust) so that I can feel better.

Being explicit takes the guessing out of a shift in posture, expression, or tone, so long as the explanation is genuine. Reporting a positive state when the internal experience is not aligned is misleading and possibly harmful as students will be picking up on nonverbal cues neuroceptively and begin to question their assessment.

## Shifting Out of Blame

**Purpose:** to shift perspective and increase curiosity and compassion when blaming self or other. To recognize blame as a defense against pain.

This exercise can be a formal reflection during times of quiet or an informal, in-the-moment practice.

When we catch ourselves judging and blaming a person for a behavior or outcome, notice the story we are telling ourselves about them.

Shift from wondering what is wrong with them to what has happened to them. Consider what painful past or present experience may be influencing behavior.

Pause and write.

Consider using a compassion practice, such as loving-kindness meditation or the "Just Like Me" exercise to connect to common humanity.

Likewise, when engaging in self-blame, shift from asking, "What's wrong with me?" to "What's happened or is happening to me?"

When we are blaming, we are suffering. Pause and reflect on the pain you are experiencing.

Pause and write.

Perhaps, use a self-compassion practice to ease your suffering.

## Default to Wonder

Adapted from school counselor, adult educator, and researcher Kim John Payne, *Being at Your Best When Your Kids Are at Their Worst: Practical Compassion in Parenting.*[18]

**Purpose:** to find and practice a go-to word or phrase for in-the-moment, stressful situations that helps you stay out of judgment.

Think of a word, phrase, sound, or mannerism that feels natural when you are relaxed, curious, and open. Consider what your body naturally moves into when you are in a state of curiosity. The response should feel genuine.

Hmm . . .

Isn't that interesting . . .

A curious tilt of the head.

The next time you find yourself in a place of judgment or blame, bring in the wondering word, sound, or mannerism. Having a reaction to default to, that keeps us in wonder, can help to replace automatic judgment and reactivity. Having a go-to mantra can interrupt reactivity, cue safety, and provide space for a more relaxed response.

# Cultivating Compassion

Though the impulse for compassion is inherent, it can be thwarted when under stress or threat. We can strengthen our ability to respond with compassion in difficult situations with deep listening, staying out of judgment, and recognizing our common humanity.

## Compassionate Listening

Adapted from Andrea S. Cohen, Susan Partnow, and Leah Green, *Practicing the Art of Compassionate Listening.*[19]

**Purpose:** to listen nonjudgmentally and with compassion without any pressure or intention to fix. To witness and fully see and hear. To be witnessed and fully seen and heard.

With a partner, think of an event that left you in mild distress or upset that you are willing to share.

Decide who will be the listener and who will be the speaker.

**Listener:** Listen deeply to the story and don't try to relate it to your own. Stay with the speaker's experience. Do not try to solve, fix, or give advice. Reflect what the speaker says, only if you need to make sure you're understanding correctly. Avoid "why" questions that can lead people back into their heads or attempt to explain. Allow silence.

**Speaker:** When conveying the experience, speak about your own feelings and experiences, not your interpretation or judgment of the "other." Tune in to your body. If you find yourself going into explanations, breathe and return to what you're feeling in the body.

Switch the role of speaker and listener.

If in a larger group, you may reflect together on what it felt like to be listened to, deeply, or to listen, deeply.

## Just Like Me

Adapted from psychologist Ram Dass and Mirabai Bush, *Walking Each Other Home: Conversations on Loving and Dying.*[20]

**Purpose:** to increase feelings of shared humanity. To connect with the humanity of another person.

This practice can be done alone, by bringing to mind a friend, a colleague, a neutral person, or a difficult person. It can also be done silently, when meeting someone new.

If working in pairs, we can practice by gazing into the eyes of another person while a third party narrates. Ask participants to sit in pairs or have them stand in two lines facing each other. Have the people look into their partners' eyes, letting them know that they can close their eyes or look down at any time if they need to.

Use any or all of the suggested phrases below or any others that may be more appropriate. Begin by becoming aware that there is a person in front of you, another human being, just like you. Then, silently repeat the phrases below, while looking at your partner.

This person has feelings, emotions, and thoughts, just like me.

This person has experienced physical and emotional pain and suffering, just like me.

This person has at some time been sad, disappointed, angry, or hurt, just like me.

This person has felt unworthy or inadequate, just like me.

This person worries and is frightened sometimes, just like me.

This person has longed for friendship, just like me.

This person is learning about life, just like me.

This person wants to be caring and kind to others, just like me.

This person wants to be content with what life has given them, just like me.

This person wishes to be free from pain and suffering, just like me.

This person wishes to be safe and healthy, just like me.

This person wishes to be happy, just like me.

This person wishes to be loved, just like me.

Thank your partner in whatever way feels appropriate.

## Loving-Kindness Meditation

From meditation teacher Sharon Salzberg, *Real Love: The Art of Mindful Connection.*[21]

**Purpose:** to cultivate compassion for self and others. To wish well-being and love for someone or for self.

Sitting comfortably, alert but relaxed, find an easy breath. You may choose to place a hand on the heart. Bring to mind a person to whom you'd like to offer compassion, kindness, or acceptance.

Holding the image of the person in your mind's eye, say these words out loud or to yourself.

"May you be safe. May you be happy. May you live with ease."

These statements may be adapted to suit your feelings and desires. Whatever well wishes you intend for the person are appropriate.

We can also send loving-kindness to ourselves.

It can be useful to begin by first sending loving-kindness to a person, animal, or being who we feel deep love for. This can conjure up the sensations in the body that come with experiencing these feelings. You may feel a warmth in the chest or other pleasurable sensation.

Focusing on that sensation, then send loving-kindness to oneself.

"May I be safe. May I be happy. May I live with ease."

Sit and breathe easily as you notice any sensations that arise.

# Self-Compassion

Recognizing and responding to our suffering can be more difficult than offering compassion to others. The impulse to be self-compassionate is not inherent. Being kind to ourselves or self-soothing can feel unnatural or counterintuitive despite the known physical and mental benefits. Fortunately, self-compassion is a skill that can be learned and practiced.

## Sending Loving-Kindness to the Inner Critic

**Purpose:** to befriend the inner critic and appreciate its role, thus allowing it to stand down.

We all have an internal critical voice. We may be aware or unaware, but it influences our feelings about ourselves. The voice may be internalized from others created in response to protect us.

Trying to ignore or stamp out the critic often makes it grow louder. Instead, we should stay curious about where it came from and how it may be trying to protect us.

Recognizing the role the inner critic plays to protect self—acknowledging, thanking, and assuring that it can stand down—shifts our perspective.

The next time we catch ourselves listening to the inner critical voice, we can give it the care it needs as a part that is suffering and doing its best to protect us. As you become aware of statements from your inner critic, rather than admonish or try to suppress or counteract those thoughts, we can befriend the critic, by acknowledging its role as protector.

Wonder what the critic may be trying to protect you from. Think of the critic as a part of you that is trying to serve you but is misguided and needs compassion. We can send loving-kindness to that part of our self.

Holding the image of a part of you that is suffering and trying to protect you, say the following.

"May you feel safe. May you feel at ease. May you know all is well.

> The transformation is not likely to happen during the practice. It happens slowly, over time, almost imperceptibly, until one day you notice that you are kinder to yourself, and the inner critic has quieted or is less critical.

## Younger Self Imagery

**Purpose:** to shift perspective to bring self-compassion when you are being especially hard on yourself. This is particularly effective when stuck in self-blame or rumination.

Reflect on the thoughts, beliefs, or harsh words you are telling yourself.

Imagine yourself as a young child. Hold the image of yourself in your mind's eye or more concretely with a physical picture of the younger self. Imagine speaking to the child with the same harsh tones and words, criticism, or blame.

Notice any feelings that arise or an urge to lessen the suffering of the child. If using the image of a younger self is too difficult, perhaps try using the imagery of a child you know and care for.

## Ideal Compassionate Other

Adapted from clinical psychologist Paul Gilbert, *The Compassionate Mind: A New Approach to Life's Challenges.*[22]

**Purpose:** to access compassion for ourselves when we have difficulty giving it to ourselves.

Sometimes we cannot access the self to give compassion to ourselves. It can be helpful to receive the care and compassion from a source you are more comfortable receiving it from. This may be any nurturing figure, past or present, such as a parent, grandparent, or other loving person you've known, or a more abstract figure, such as a spiritual figure. Or you might choose a field of light or a part of nature that represents wisdom, knowing, strength, and stability, such as an old tree or a flowing stream that can give you the compassionate presence.

By imagining the compassion and protection coming from the wise figure or from nature, we practice activating our self-soothing system. We feel cared for.

The figure is wise, warm, nonjudgmental. The part of nature is neutral, calming, and supportive.

Some people prefer an image over a human figure. Especially those who find human images too threatening, or perhaps have no person, real or imagined, to anchor these self-soothing feelings.

## Self-Compassion for Needs

Adapted from Tibetan Buddhist scholar and former monk Thupten Jinpa, *A Fearless Heart: How the Courage to Be Compassionate Can Transform Our Lives.*[23]

**Purpose:** to shift out of self-blame or shame. To practice recognizing our needs that underlie unwanted behavior. To bring kindness, compassion, and forgiveness to ourselves.

Think of a time when you did something that you wish you hadn't and, as a result, you reproached yourself for it.

Recalling specifics is not necessary unless they help you to evoke the emotional reaction you felt then.

What is important is the recollection of how you engaged in negative self-judgment. Stay with this reflection.

Then ask yourself, "Why is it that I reacted so harshly then? What was the unmet need I was trying to fulfill when I did this thing?"

Stay with these reflections for a little while.

Now recognize that although what you did was not skillful, the underlying need that prompted your action was legitimate.

With awareness, allow yourself to experience feelings such as sadness, disappointment, and remorse, rather than guilt and shame. Pause with these feelings.

Notice any tension in your body.

Now breathing out slowly and completely, let go of any tension in the body,

Let go silently. Say to yourself, "I can let this go. I will let it go."

Imagine feeling free. Expand your chest and breathe out fully a few more times.

# Endnotes

**Overview**
1. Porges (2011, 2017, pp. 218–219); Twemlow (2002)
2. Porges (2007, 2011, 2017, pp. 19–20)
3. Porges (2017, p. 7, pp. 48–50)
4. Powell et al. (2014, p. 48)
5. Porges (2011, 2017, pp. 100–102)
6. Tronick (1989); Tronick and Beeghly (2011)
7. Rosenberg (2015)

**Part I Shifting School Culture**
1. Brouwers and Tomic (2000)
2. Powell et al. (2014, p. 48)
3. Porges (2011, 2017, pp. 48–50)
4. Siegel (1999)
5. Tronick (1989); Tronick and Beeghly (2011)
6. Ratey (2008)
7. Porges (2017)
8. Bouwers and Tomic (2000)
9. Gilbert (2007)
10. Schore (2013)
11. Slade (2005)
12. Porges (2017, pp. 48–50)
13. Baumann et al. (2001)
14. Herman (2002)
15. OSEP (2021)
16. Bowlby (1988)
17. Porges (2017)
18. Neff et al., (2009)
19. Porges (2017)
20. Dana (2018, p. 6)
21. Perry and Szalavitz (2017, p. 308)
22. Porges (2017, pp. 48–49)
23. Debarnot et al. (2014); Buckner et al. (2008); Schuster et al. (2011)
24. Brown (2016)
25. McAdams (2001)
26. Rosenthal and Jacobson (1968)
27. Rosenberg (2015)
28. Rosenberg (2015)

**Part II Resourcing the Educator**
1. Porges (2017)
2. Mason et al. (2007); Buckner et al. (2008)
3. Mason et al. (2007); Buckner et al. (2008)
4. Mason et al. (2007); Buckner et al. (2008)
5. Brewer et al. (2013) Northoff et al. (2006)

6. Chun et al. (2007)
7. Brewer et al. (2013)
8. Hebb (1949)
9. Kabat-Zinn (2013)
10. Holzel et al. (2010); Holzel et al. (2011)
11. Holzel et al. (2010)
12. James (1894)
13. Bull (1951)
14. Ekman (1992); Cuddy et al. (2018); McIntosh (1996)
15. Ekman (1992)
16. McIntosh (1996)
17. Carney et al. (2010); Cuddy et al. (2018)
18. Chodron (2013)
19. Nair et al. (1994)
20. Porges (2007, 2017)
21. Siegel (1999)
22. Payne (2019)
23. Dana (2018, 6); (Porges 2017, 148)
24. Ledoux (1977)
25. Nisbett and Wilson (1977)
26. Baumann et al., (2001)
27. Debarnot et al. (2014)
28. McGonigal (2015)
29. www.developingchild.harvard.edu
30. www.developingchild.harvard.edu
31. Jamieson et al. (2012)
32. Pert (1997)
33. Brouwers and Tomic (2000)
34. Powell et al. (2014)
35. Garbarino (1999)
36. Crenshaw and Garbarino (2007)
37. Palmer and Crawford (2013)
38. Porges (2017)
39. Klimicki et al. (2014)
40. Brouwer and Tomic (2000)
41. Goetz et al. (2010)
42. Klimicki et al. (2014)
43. Klimicki et al. (2014)
44. Gilbert (2009)
45. Darley and Batson (1973)
46. Bachner-Melman and Ebstein (2014)
47. Carter (2014)
48. Bachner-Melman and Ebstein (2014)
49. Goetz et al. (2010)
50. Neff (2003a, 2003b)
51. Neff et al. (2005)
52. Williams et al. (2008)

53. Brienes and Chen (2012)
54. Neely et al. (2009)
55. Neely et al. (2009)
56. Gilbert (2007)
57. Cozolino (2013)
58. Gilbert (2007); Cozolino (2013)
59. Gilbert (2009)
60. Jinpa (2015)

**Part III  Practices to Resource the Educator**
1. Barrett et al. (2004)
2. Carney et al. (2010); Porges (2017)
3. Lesser (2004)
4. Carney et al. (2010)
5. Porges (2011)
6. UCLAhealth.org/marc/
7. Courtney et al. (2011)
8. Courtney et al. (2011)
9. HeartMath.org
10. Jerath et al. (2006); Busch et al. (2012); Kuppusamy (2018)
11. Levine (2010, pp. 126–127)
12. Bratmana (2015); Ulrich et al. (1991)
13. Berman et al. (2012); Taylor et al. (2002)
14. Hartig et al. (2014)
15. Brown (2013)
16. Rosenberg (2015)
17. Palmer and Crawford (2013)
18. Payne (2019)
19. Cohen et al. (2011)
20. Dass and Bush (2018)
21. Salzburg (2017)
22. Gilbert (2007 p. 256)
23. Jinpa (2015)

# *References*

Bachner-Melman, R., and Ebstein, R. P. (2014). "The Role of Oxytocin and Vasopressin in Emotional and Social Behaviors." *Handbook of Clinical Neurology* 124: 53–68. doi: 10.1016/B978-0-444-59602-4.00004-6.

Barrett, L.F., Quigley, K.S., Bliss-Moreau, E., and Aronson, K.R. (2004). "Interoceptive Sensitivity and Self-Reports of Emotional Experience." *Journal of Personality and Social Psychology* 87(5): 684–697.

Baumann, M.R., Sniezek, J.A, and Buerkle, C.A. (2001). "Self-Evaluation, Stress, and Performance: A Model of Decision Making under Acute Stress." In E. Salas and G. Klein (eds.), *Linking Expertise and Naturalistic Decision Making* (139–158). Lawrence Erlbaum Associates Publishers.

Berman, M.G., Kross, E., Krpan, K.M., Askren, M.K., Burson, A., Deldin, P.J., Kaplan, S., Sherdell, L., Gotlib, I.H., and Jonides, J. (2012). Interacting with Nature Improves Cognition and Affect for Individuals with Depression." *Journal of Affective Disorders* 140(3): 300–305. doi.org/10.1016/j.jad.2012.03.012.

Bowlby, J. (1988). *A Secure Base: Parent-Child Attachment and Healthy Human Development.* New York, New York: Basic Books.

Bratmana, G.N., Hamilton, J.P., Hahn, K.S., Daily, G.C., and Gross, J.J. (2015). "Nature Experience Reduces Rumination and Subgenual Prefrontal Cortex Activation." *Proc Natl Acad Sci* 112(28): 8567–8572. doi: 10.1073/pnas.1510459112.

Breines, J.G., and Chen, S. (2012). "Self-Compassion Increases Self-Improvement Motivation. *Personality and Social Psychology Bulletin* 20(10): 1–11. doi: 10.1177/0146167212445599.

Brewer, J.A., Garrison, K.A., and Whitfield-Gabrieli, S. (2013). What about the "Self" Is Processed in the Posterior Cingulate Cortex?" *Frontiers in Human Neuroscience* 7(647): 1–7.

Brouwers, A., and Tomic, W. (2000). "A Longitudinal Study of Teacher Burnout and Perceived Self-Efficacy in Classroom Management." *Teaching and Teacher Education* 16(2): 239–253. PII: S0742-051X(99)00057-8.

Brown, D. (2016). *Meditation for Everyday Living and Peak Performance.* Conference held at the Fairmont, Boston, Massachusetts, December 3–4.

Brown, D.K., Barton, J.L., Gladwell, V.F. (2013). "Viewing Nature Scenes Positively Affects Recovery of Autonomic Function Following Acute-Mental Stress." *Environmental Science and Technology* 47: 5562–5569. dx.doi.org/10.1021/es305019p.

Buckner, R.L., Andrews-Hanna, J.R., Schacter, D.L. (2008). "The Brain's Default Network: Anatomy, Function, and Relevance to Disease." *Annals NY Acad Sci.* 1124: 1–38.

Bull, N. (1951). *The Attitude Theory of Emotion.* Nervous and Mental Disease Monograph.

Busch, V., Magerl, W., Kern, U., Haas, J., Hajak, G., and Eichhammer, P. (2012). The Effect of Deep and Slow Breathing on Pain Perception, Autonomic Activity, and Mood Processing—An Experimental Study. *Pain Med.* 13: 215–228. 10.1111/j.1526-4637.2011.01243.x.

Carney, D.R., Cuddy, A.J.C., and Yap, A.J. (2010). "Power Posing: Brief Nonverbal Displays Affect Neuroendocrine Levels and Risk Tolerance." *Psychological Science* 21(10): 1363–1368.

Carter, C.S., Bantal, I.B., and Porges, E.C. (2017). "The Roots of Compassion: An Evolutionary and Neurobiological Perspective," Chapter 14. *The Oxford Handbook of Compassion Science.* Emma M. Seppälä, Emiliana Simon-Thomas, Stephanie L. Brown, Monica C. Worline, C. Daryl Cameron, and James R. Doty (eds).

Chodron, P. (2013). *How to Meditate: A Practical Guide to Making Friends with Your Mind.* Boulder, Colorado: Sounds True, Inc.

Chun, M.M., and Turk-Browne, N.B. (2007). "Interactions between Attention and Memory." *Current Opinion in Neurobiology* 17(2): 177–184. doi.org/10.1016/j.conb.2007.03.005.

Cohen, A.S., Partnow, S., and Green, L. (2011). *Practicing the Art of Compassionate Listening.* The Compassionate Listening Project.

Courtney, R., Cohen, M., and van Dixhoorn, J. (2011). "Relationship between Dysfunctional Breathing Patterns and Ability to Achieve Target Heart Rate Variability with Features of 'Coherence' during Biofeedback." *Alternative Therapies in Health Medicine* 17(3): 38–44. PMID: 22164811.

Cozolino, L. (2013). *The Social Neuroscience of Education: Optimizing Attachment and Learning in the Classroom.* New York: W.W. Norton and Co.

Crenshaw, D.A., and Garbarino, J. (2007). "The Hidden Dimensions: Profound Sorrow and Buried Potential in Violent Youth." *Journal of Humanistic Psychology* 47(2): 160–174. doi.org/10.1177/0022167806293310.

Cuddy, A.J., Schultz, S.J., and Fosse, N.E. (2018). "P-Curving a More Comprehensive Body of Research on Postural Feedback Reveals Clear Evidential Value for Power-Posing Effects: Reply to Simmons and Simonsohn (2017). *Psychological Science* 29(4): 656–666. doi: 10.1177/0956797617746749.

Dana, D. (2018). *The Polyvagal Theory in Therapy: Engaging the Rhythm of Regulation.* New York, New York: W.W. Norton and Co.

Darley, J. M., and Batson, C.D. (1973). "'From Jerusalem to Jericho': A Study of Situational and Dispositional Variables in Helping Behavior." *Journal of Personality and Social Psychology* 27: 100–108.

Dass, R., and Bush, M. (2018). *Walking Each Other Home: Conversations on Loving and Dying.* Sounds True, Inc.

Debarnot, U., Sperduti, M., Di Rienzo, F., and Guillot, A. (2014). "Experts' Bodies, Experts' Minds: How Physical and Mental Training Shape the Brain." *Frontiers in*

*Human Neuroscience* 8: 280. doi: 10.3389/fnhum.2014.00280.

Ekman, P. (1992). "An Argument for Basic Emotions." *Cognition and Emotion* 6(3/4): 169–200.

Garbarino, J. (1999). *Lost Boys: Why Our Sons Turn Violent and How We Can Save Them.* New York, New York: Simon and Schuster.

Gilbert, P. (2007). "The Evolution of Shame as a Marker for Relationship Security: A Biopsychosocial Approach." In J.L. Tracy, R.W. Robins, and J.P. Tangney (eds.), *The Self-Conscious Emotions: Theory and Research* (283–309). Guilford Press.

Gilbert, P. (2009). *The Compassionate Mind: A New Approach to Life's Challenges.* Oakland, California: New Harbinger.

Goetz, J.L., Keltner, D., and Simon-Thomas, E. (2010). "Compassion: An Evolutionary Analysis and Empirical Review." *Psychol Bulletin* 136(3): 351–374. doi:10.1037/a0018807.

Hartig, T., Mitchell, R., de Vries, S., and Frumkin, H. (2014). "Nature and Health." *Annu Rev Public Health* 35: 207–228.

Hebb, D.O. (1949). *The Organization of Behavior: A Neuropsychological Theory.* New York: Wiley.

Herman, J.L. (2002). "Recovery from Psychological Trauma." *Psychiatry and Clinical Neurosciences* 52(S1):S98-S103.

Holzel, B.K., Carmody, J., Evans, K.C., Hoge, E.A., Dusek, J.A., Morgan, L., Pitman, R.K., and Lazar, S.W. (2010). "Stress Reduction Correlates with Structural Changes in the Amygdala." *SCAN* (5): 11–17.

Holzel, B.K., Carmody, J., Vangel, M., Congleton, C., Yerramsetti, S.M., Gard, T., and Lazar, S. (2011). "Mindfulness Practice Leads to Increases in Regional Brain Gray Matter Density." *Psychiatry Res.* 191: 36–43. 10.1016/j.pscychresns.2010.08.006.

James, W. (1894). "Discussion: The Physical Basis of Emotion." *Psychological Review* 1(5): 516–529.

Jamieson, J.P., Nock, M.K., Mendes, W.B. (2012). "Mind over Matter: Reappraising Arousal Improves Cardiovascular and Cognitive Responses to Stress." *Journal of Experimental Psychology General* 141(3): 417–422. doi:10.1037/a0025719.

Jerath, R., Edry, J.W., Barnes, V.A., and Jerath V. (2006). "Physiology of Long Pranayamic Breathing: Neural Respiratory Elements May Provide a Mechanism That Explains How Slow Deep Breathing Shifts the Autonomic Nervous System." *Med. Hypotheses* 67: 566–571. 10.1016/j.mehy.2006.02.042.

Jinpa, T. (2015). *A Fearless Heart: How the Courage to Be Compassionate Can Transform Our Lives.* New York, New York: Penguin Random House.

Kabat-Zinn, J. (2013). *Full Catastrophe Living: Using the Wisdom of Your Body and Mind to Face Stress, Pain, and Illness.* New York: Bantam Dell.

Kaplan, R. (2001). "The Nature of the View from Home." *Environ Behav* 33(4): 507–542.

Klimecki, O.M., Leiberg, S., Ricard, M., and Singer, T. (2014). "Differential Pattern of Functional Brain Plasticity after Compassion and Empathy Training." *Social Cognitive and Affective Neuroscience* 9: 873–879.

Kuppusamy, M., Kamaldeen, D., Pitani, R., Amaldas, J., and Shanmugam, P. (2018). "Effects of Bhramari Pranayama on Health: A Systematic Review." *Journal of Traditional and Complementary Medicine* 8: 11–16.

LeDoux, J.E., Wilson, D.H., and Gazzaniga, M.S. (1977). "A Divided Mind: Observations on the Conscious Properties of the Separated Hemispheres." *Annals of Neurology* 2(5): 417–421 PMID: 103484.

Lesser, E. (2008). *Broken Open: How Difficult Times Can Help Us Grow.* New York, New York: Villard.

Levine, P.A. (2010). *In an Unspoken Voice: How the Body Releases Trauma and Restores Goodness.* Berkeley, California: North Atlantic Books.

Mason, M.F., Norton, M.I., Van Horn, J.D., Wegner, D.M., Grafton, S.T., and Macrae, C.N. (2007). "Wandering Minds: The Default Network and Stimulus Independent Thought." *Science* 315: 393–395.

McAdams, DP. (2001). "The Psychology of Life Stories." Review of General Psychology 5: 100–122.

McGonigal, K. (2015). *The Upside of Stress: Why Stress Is Good for You, and How to Get Good at It.* New York: Penguin Random House.

McIntosh, D.N. (1996). "Facial Feedback Hypotheses: Evidence, Implications, and Directions." *Motivation and Emotion* 20(2): 121–147.

Nair, S., Sagar, M., Sollers III, J., Consedine, N., and Broadbent, E. (2015). "Do Slumped and Upright Postures Affect Stress Responses? A Randomized Trial." *Health Psychology* 34(6): 632–641. https://doi.org/10.1037/hea0000146.

Neely, M.R., Schallert, D.J., Mohammed, S.S., Roberts, R.M., and Chen, Y. (2009). "Self-Kindness When Facing Stress: The Role of Self-Compassion, Goal Regulation, and Support in College Students' Well-Being." *Motivation and Emotion* 33: 88–97.

Neff, K.D. (2003a). "The Development and Validation of a Scale to Measure Self-Compassion." *Self and Identity* 2: 223–250. doi:http://dx.doi.org/10.1080/15298860390209035.

Neff, K.D. (2003b). "Self-Compassion: An Alternative Conceptualization of a Healthy Attitude toward Oneself." *Self and Identity* 2: 85–101. doi:http://dx.doi.org/10.1080/15298860309032.

Neff, K.D., and Vonk, R. (2009). "Self-Compassion Versus Global Self-Esteem: Two Different Ways of Relating to Oneself." *Journal of Personality* 77: 23–50.

Neff, K.D., Hsieh, Y., and Dejitterat, K. (2005). "Self-Compassion, Achievement Goals, and Coping with Academic Failure." *Self and Identity* 4: 263–287. doi:http://dx.doi.org/10.1080/13576500444000317.

Nisbett, R., and Wilson, T. (1977). "Telling More Than We Can Know: Verbal Reports on Mental Processes." *Psychological Review* 84(3): 231–259. doi: 10.1037//0033-295X.84.3.231.

Northoff, G., Heinzel, A., de Greck, M., Bermpohl, F., Dobrowolny, H., Panksepp, J. (2006). "Self-Referential Processing in Our Brain—A Meta-Analysis of Imaging Studies on the Self." *Neuroimage* 31: 440–457.

OSEP Technical Assistance Center on Positive Behavioral Interventions and Supports. (2021). Positive Behavioral Interventions & Supports. www.pbis.org.

Palmer, W., and Crawford, J. (2013). *Leadership Embodiment: How the Way We Sit and Stand Can Change the Way We Think and Speak.* CreateSpace.

Payne, K.J., (2019). *Being at Your Best When Your Kids Are at Their Worst: Practical Compassion in Parenting.* Boulder, Colorado: Shambhala Publications.

Perry, B.D., and Szalavitz, M. (2017). The Boy Who Was Raised as a Dog: And Other Stories from a Child Psychiatrist's Notebook—What Traumatized Children Can Teach Us about Loss, Love, and Healing. New York: Basic Books.

Pert, C. (1997). *Molecules of Emotion: The Science Behind Mind-Body Medicine.* New York, New York: Simon and Schuster.

Porges, S. (2017). *The Pocket Guide to the Polyvagal Theory: The Transformative Power of Feeling Safe.* New York: W.W. Norton and Co.

Porges, S.W. (2007). "The Polyvagal Perspective." *Biol. Psychol.* 74: 116–143. 10.1016/j.biopsycho.2006.06.009.

Porges, S.W. (2011a). *The Polyvagal Theory: Neurophysiological Foundations of Emotions, Attachment, Communication, and Self-Regulation.* New York: W.W. Norton and Co.

Powell, B., Cooper, G., Hoffman, K., and Marvin, B. (2014). *The Circle of Security Intervention: Enhancing Attachment in Early Parent-Child Relationships.* New York: The Guilford Press.

Ratey, J. (2008). *Spark: The Revolutionary New Science of Exercise and the Brain.* New York, New York: Little, Brown, and Co.

Rosenberg, M. (2015). *Nonviolent Communication: A Language of Life: Life-Changing Tools for Healthy Relationships,* Edition 3, Encinitas, California: Puddledancer Press.

Rosenthal, R., and Jacobson, L. (1968). "Pygmalion in the Classroom." *Urban Rev* 3: 16–20. https://doi.org/10.1007/BF02322211.

Salzberg, S. (2017). *Real Love: The Art of Mindful Connection.* New York, New York: Flatiron Books.

Schore, A. (2013). "Allan Schore Neurobiology of Secure Attachment.f4v." www.youtube.com/watch?v=WVuJ5KhpL34 www.youtube.com/watch?v=LpHpm_b0vRY.

Schuster, C., Hilfiker, R., Amft, O., Scheidhauer, A., Andrews, B., Butler, J., Kischka, U., and Ettlin, T. (2011). "Best Practice for Motor Imagery: A Systematic Literature Review on Motor Imagery Training Elements in Five Different Disciplines." *BMC Med.* 9(75). doi: 10.1186/1741-7015-9-75.

Siegel, D.J. (1999). "Memory." In *The Developing Mind: How Relationships and the Brain Interact to Shape Who We Are,* 23–66, New York: Guilford Press.

Slade, A. (2005). "Parental Reflective Functioning: An Introduction." *Attachment and Human Development* 7(3): 269–281.

Taylor, A.F., Kuo, F.E., and Sullivan, W.C. (2002). "Views of Nature and Self-Discipline: Evidence from Inner City Children." *Journal of Environmental Psychology* 22(1–2): 49–63.

Tronick, E. (1989). "Emotions and Emotional Communication in Infants." *American Psychologist.* Special Issue: Children and Their Development: Knowledge Base, Research Agenda, and Social Policy Application. 44(2): 112–119.

Tronick, E., and Beeghley, M. (2011). "Infants' Meaning-Making and the Development of Mental Health Problems." *American Psychologist* 66(2): 107–119. doi:10.1037/a0021631.

Twemlow, S.W., Fonagy, P., and Sacco, F.C. (2002). "Feeling Safe in School." *Smith College Studies in Social Work* 72(2): 303–326. doi: 10.1080/00377310209517660.

Ulrich, R., Simons, R.F., Losito, B.D., Fiorito E., Miles, M.A., and Zelson, M. (1991). "Stress Recovery during Exposure to Natural and Urban Environments." *Journal of Environmental Psychology* 11(3): 201–230. doi.org/10.1016/S0272-4944(05)80184-7.

Williams, J.G., Stark, S.K., and Foster, E.E. (2008). "Start Today or the Very Last Day? The Relationships among Self-Compassion, Motivation, and Procrastination." *American Journal of Psychological Research* 4: 37–44.

www.ingramcontent.com/pod-product-compliance
Lightning Source LLC
Chambersburg PA
CBHW022105040426
42451CB00007B/135